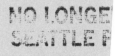

PRAISE FOR

The Populist Explosion

The Nationalist Revival

"Excellent and compact book. . . . A person of the left, Judis specializes in speaking truth to liberals, something he also did in his earlier *The Populist Explosion*. He thinks it's important for progressives to understand why so many are drawn to Trump and the far right in Europe."

E.J. DIONNE JR.
Washington Post

"John B. Judis does not see a death-match between imperial liberalism on the one hand and nationalism on the other. His book argues that elites have overreached, both in the U.S. and in Europe, in advocating large-scale immigration and trade deals and foreign interventions."

JASON WILLICK
Wall Street Journal

"John B. Judis is the rare left-of-center journalist who takes our populist-nationalist moment seriously. Rather than dismiss the leaders and constituencies of the American and European movements as mere xenophobes, he offers an empathetic balls-and-strikes analysis of the socioeconomic factors that made—and continue to make—such campaigns viable."

DANIEL KISHI
The American Conservative

The Socialist Awakening
What's Different Now
About the Left

COLUMBIA GLOBAL REPORTS
NEW YORK

The Socialist Awakening

What's Different Now About the Left

John B. Judis

United
States

United
Kingdom

© 2020 Jeffrey L. Ward

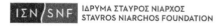

ΙΔΡΥΜΑ ΣΤΑΥΡΟΣ ΝΙΑΡΧΟΣ
STAVROS NIARCHOS FOUNDATION

Published with support from the Stavros Niarchos Foundation (SNF)

The Socialist Awakening:
What's Different Now About the Left
Copyright © 2020 by John B. Judis
All rights reserved

Published by Columbia Global Reports
91 Claremont Avenue, Suite 515
New York, NY 10027
globalreports.columbia.edu
facebook.com/columbiaglobalreports
@columbiaGR

Library of Congress Cataloging-in-Publication Data
Description: New York, NY : Columbia Global Reports, [2020] | Includes
    bibliographical references.
Identifiers: LCCN 2020028631 (print) | LCCN 2020028632 (ebook) | ISBN
    9781734420708 (paperback) | ISBN 9781734420715 (ebook)
Subjects: LCSH: Socialism--United States--History--21st century. | Socialism--
    Great Britain--History--21st century.
Classification: LCC HX86 .J83 2020 (print) | LCC HX86 (ebook) | DDC
    320.53/10973--dc23
LC record available at https://lccn.loc.gov/2020028631
LC ebook record available at https://lccn.loc.gov/2020028632

Book design by Strick&Williams
Map design by Jeffrey L. Ward
Author photograph by Miranda Sita

Printed in the United States of America

For Shelly Weintraub and Tim Reagan

CONTENTS

Socialism Old
and New

The philosopher Fredric Jameson once wrote, "It is easier to imagine the end of the world than to imagine the end of capitalism." Jameson, hardly known as a staunch defender of capitalism (he's perhaps the world's foremost Marxist literary critic), didn't write this generations ago, but in 2003. In March 2020, as the novel coronavirus outbreak was putting millions of Americans under stay-at-home orders, and as Congress and the Federal Reserve had begun pouring trillions of dollars into the economy to soften the blow of a coming depression, Vox editor Dylan Matthews quipped: "The end of the world is making it easier to imagine the end of capitalism."

The coronavirus pandemic came barely five years after the United States and Western Europe were finally recovering from the Great Recession of 2008. It has not, and will not, spell the end of the world or of capitalism, but it has put the final nail in the coffin of the laissez-faire, globalized capitalism that prevailed since the days of Margaret Thatcher and Ronald Reagan and that was perpetuated, wittingly or not, by their successors.

16   The era of big government, which Bill Clinton claimed was over under his watch, is back with a vengeance; and so is the attention of politicians, if only for the time being, to the welfare of the many, not just the few.

The politics and political economy in the United States and Europe (not to mention elsewhere) are entering a new era, just as it happened in the early 1930s, after World War II, and then again in the early 1980s. In the early 1930s, faced with the breakdown of the gold-based international monetary system and of untamed capitalism at home, the countries of the West went in very different directions. The United States went toward Franklin Roosevelt's New Deal; Central and Southern Europe went toward Nazism and fascism. Both alternatives, as socialist theorist Karl Polanyi described them in *The Great Transformation*, were attempts to use the power of government to protect the populace against the vicissitudes of the market.

The failure of market capitalism has been heightened by the threat posed by the novel coronavirus. All the weaknesses of the previous era—from the over-reliance on global supply chains to underfunded social services; from tax avoidance by the wealthy and large corporations to the immiseration of what are known as "essential workers"—have been laid bare. And after the threat of the virus recedes, the countries of the world will still face steep unemployment and a daunting task of economic reconstruction, along with the growing threat of climate change, that will require major public initiatives. These failures and weaknesses can be, as they were in the United States in the 1930s, the basis for a traditional leftwing alliance of the bottom and the middle of society against the very top. Or they can feed rightwing attempts to divide the middle and bottom through scapegoating.

Even before the current pandemic and depression, the breakdown in the older economic consensus had resulted in new and sometimes unforeseen political eruptions. Many of these occurred on the right, through the rise of a toxic "us vs. them" nationalist politics in the United States and Europe, and the move toward authoritarianism in Eastern Europe, Turkey, and India and toward a new cyber-totalitarianism in China. There have also, however, been unexpected flare-ups on the political left and center-left. These include a leftwing populism in Southern Europe, the rise of the Greens on the European continent, the attempt by Britain's Labour Party to revive its commitment to socialism, and the awakening in the United States, the bastion of Cold War anti-communism, of a new socialist politics.

The principal subject of this book is the rise of a socialist politics in the United States and the failed attempt to revive socialism in Great Britain. Like my previous books on populism and nationalism, I will try to describe and explain these political phenomena. But as a longtime leftist who labored unsuccessfully decades ago trying to create a socialist movement in the United States, and whose hopes for a socialist politics have been rekindled by the Bernie Sanders campaigns, I have definite views on what socialists should and should not do to build a viable movement.

In the United States, the revival of interest in socialism has been due to Sanders, who, when he began running for president in 2015, was little known except in Vermont and on the left, and

18   was disdained by some of his colleagues in Congress. Running as a "democratic socialist," he almost won against prohibitive favorite Hillary Clinton. Four years later, Sanders again came in second, consistently winning the greatest share of voters under age forty-five—voters who hadn't grown up in the shadow of the Cold War and with the identification of socialism with Soviet communism. In an October 2019 YouGov poll, 70 percent of millennials (ages 23–38) said they were "extremely" or "somewhat likely" to vote for a socialist.

Sanders's failure to win the nomination was predictable, as there are still too many older Americans who associate socialism with the Soviet Union. But Sanders's campaigns had a dramatic influence on the Democratic Party's agenda. A host of Democrats embraced his plan for a single-payer healthcare system and his proposal to raise the minimum wage to $15 an hour. Senate Minority Leader Chuck Schumer, not known as a democratic socialist, embraced Sanders's plan to put workers on corporate boards. And Joe Biden, who bested Sanders for the nomination, gave key Sanders supporters prominent places on his policy task forces and crafted a campaign platform that reflected Sanders's influence.

The Democratic Socialists of America (DSA) has grown rapidly. In 2015, DSA had 6,000 members. A year after Sanders's campaign, DSA's membership had quintupled. After DSA member Alexandria Ocasio-Cortez's election to Congress in 2018, it rose to 56,000, making it the largest democratic socialist organization since the pre–World War I Socialist Party. In the wake of the pandemic and depression, it has grown to 70,000. DSA also boasts over a hundred officeholders. If the United States had a multi-party system with proportional voting, a democratic socialist party might command a very respectable 15 to 20 percent of the vote.

The young people who have taken a positive view of socialism don't necessarily have a worked-out theory of socialism or socialist politics. In the United States, they often identify socialism with Scandinavian countries, and with public control of healthcare, education, and energy. They condemn the growing inequality of wealth and power and want a society based on cooperation rather than on cutthroat competition and on sexual and racial equality. They don't envisage the government owning Apple or Microsoft. Sanders's own explanation of democratic socialism runs along these same lines.

Some commentators have insisted that neither Sanders nor his young supporters are really socialists. To be a socialist, columnist Eric Levitz wrote in *New York*, is to advocate "the abolition of profit or worker ownership of the means of production." Paul Krugman defined socialists as people who want to "nationalize our major industries and replace markets with central planning." But that is not what the rising popular sympathy for democratic socialism is about. Socialism is coming back in a form that is different not only from the Soviet Union's or Cuba's communism, but from what socialists who consider themselves to be "Marxists" have envisaged. And it could play an important role in shaping voters' reaction to what has been the greatest threat to Americans' well-being since the Great Depression and World War II.

The Varieties of Socialist Experience
Just as there is no exclusive definition of populism, liberalism, or conservatism, there is no singular definition of socialism.

20   According to Marxist theorist Raymond Williams's *Keywords: A Vocabulary of Culture and Society*, the term "socialism" first appeared in English in the 1820s and its French counterpart, "socialisme," in the 1830s. Some thinkers were described as "socialists" who merely concerned themselves with social matters, similar to what a sociologist would do today. But in its critical use, it referred to thinkers who rejected the competitive individualism of industrial capitalism. Socialism was paired against individualism; cooperation against competition; altruism against selfishness. It was initially inspired by the spirit of the American Revolution ("all men are created equal") and the French Revolution ("Liberty, equality, fraternity") and by the ethics of the Sermon on the Mount. Over the subsequent centuries, it has taken at least five different forms, only one of which comes directly out of the work of Karl Marx.

Utopian Socialism: In the first half of the nineteenth century, Charles Fourier, Robert Owen, Pierre Joseph-Proudhon, and Henri de Saint-Simon were all described as socialists primarily on the basis of their rejection of competitive individualism. In his *New Christianity*, Saint-Simon advocated a spirit of association and obligation toward the poor. Owen, a Welsh textile manufacturer, sought to replace the prevailing factory system with a communal system, which he called "villages of cooperation," where workers would live and be fed and have their children educated. Fourier advocated communes called "phalansteries." Proudhon backed workers' cooperatives and a philosophy he called "mutualism." Fourier, Owen, and Saint-Simon hoped to spread socialism by example. Industrialists and workers would see that cooperative production was not only morally superior, but more efficient.

Christian or Ethical Socialism: The Utopian Socialists like Saint-Simon were influenced by Christian ideals, but there were a host of Christian socialists in the mid-nineteenth century who traced their views directly to the gospel. They included Philippe Buchez, who was a member of the Saint-Simon Society, and Anglo-Indian lawyer John Malcolm Ludlow, who founded a Christian Socialist movement in England in the late 1840s that advocated giving "the kingdom of Christ . . . the true authority over the realms of industry and trade" and "for socialism its true character as the great Christian revolution." In the United States, Walter Rauschenbusch and a young Reinhold Niebuhr played prominent roles in promoting Christian socialism. Like Marxist socialism, it had an apocalyptic, millennial element, expressed in the idea of creating the Kingdom of God on Earth.

Orthodox Marxism: From the 1890s, when Marx's and Engels's theories became the official doctrine of Europe's leading socialist party, the German Social Democratic Party (SPD), Marxism became the touchstone for many socialists in the West. If you were a serious and not merely a nominal socialist, you were a Marxist. Marx's and Engels's own theories changed over their lifetimes, but there was a core orthodox doctrine that became the starting point for many discussions of socialism. It was most clearly articulated by SPD leader Karl Kautsky in *The Class Struggle.*

According to orthodox Marxism, history was divided into distinct stages defined by relations of production (classes) and forces of production (technology) and punctuated by revolutionary upheavals. Capitalism had succeeded feudalism, and socialism would succeed capitalism. It would be characterized by social ownership and control of the means of production; the disappearance of a capitalist class, markets, and money; and social and economic equality.

The revolution would be led by a homogeneous blue-collar working class, which as a result of industrialization, would encompass the majority of workers and would be conscious of itself as an oppressed class. Organized into unions and parties, it would respond to growing economic crises and to its own immiseration by overthrowing capitalism and establishing socialism. The revolution would be international ("Workers of the world, unite!") and would eventually result in the dissolution of national borders.

Marx and Engels drew a distinction between "utopian" and "scientific" socialism. "Utopian" socialism was based on wishful thinking and the power of example. By contrast, "scientific" socialism was rooted in inexorable historical trends that would make the fall of capitalism inevitable. But Marx's and Engels's scenario for the transition from capitalism to socialism never came to pass. Capitalism has not succumbed to collapse and socialist revolution. There is much to learn from their analysis of capitalism and of the transition from feudalism to capitalism, but the Marx and Engels's view of socialism and of socialist politics proved to be as "utopian" as Owen's, Fourier's, and Saint-Simon's.

In retrospect, it appears that Marxist socialism was heavily influenced by Judeo-Christian eschatology. In *Meaning in History*, German philosopher Karl Lowith contended that in *The Communist Manifesto*, Marx was unconsciously mimicking the Judeo-Christian portrayal of the end times—Armageddon leading to the Millennium—in his account of a revolutionary class struggle that would culminate in pure communism and the withering away of the state. Marx and Engels were, of course, atheists, but that doesn't preclude their having unconsciously framed their theory of history and politics in biblical terms.* Indeed, many socialist or communist organizations have unconsciously mimicked the behavior of Protestant sects.

Marxism-Leninism: Soviet dictator Josef Stalin promoted a distinct doctrine he called "Marxism-Leninism" after he seized power in 1928. Stalin foresaw a prolonged period of transition between capitalism and socialism characterized by "the dictatorship of the proletariat." Marx had used the term ironically—his model was the democratically elected Paris Commune of

---

* Lowith writes: "It is therefore not by chance that the 'last' antagonism between the two hostile camps of bourgeoisie and proletariat corresponds to the Jewish-Christian belief in a final fight between Christ and Antichrist in the last epoch of history, that the task of the proletariat corresponds to the world-historical mission of the chosen people, that the redemptive and universal function of the most degraded class is conceived on the religious pattern of Cross and Resurrection, that the ultimate transformation of the realm of necessity into a realm of freedom corresponds to the transformation of the civitas Terrena [city of man] into civitas Dei [city of God], and that the whole process of history as outlined in the Communist Manifesto corresponds to the general scheme of the Jewish-Christian interpretation of history as a providential advance toward a final goal which is meaningful."

1871—but Stalin used it to justify the dictatorial control of the state by the Communist Party, which could use its control in order to extirpate the enemies of socialism. Marxism-Leninism also came to be associated with Lenin's idea of the party as a disciplined elite (the "cadre") that knew the interests of the working class better than the working class itself did.

Against the orthodox Marxist that socialism could only develop in advanced economies, or in tandem with other advanced economies, Stalin argued that socialism and the transition to communism could occur within an individual, less developed nation. China's and Vietnam's parties continue to use Marxism-Leninism to justify their dominance. And versions of Marxism-Leninism have popped up to justify regimes in Cuba and Venezuela.

During the sixties, some new left groups adopted independent versions of Marxist-Leninism that incorporated what they believed to be Mao Zedong Thought. In the United States, the Black Panther Party anointed Stalin's *Foundations of Leninism* as its guide to revolutionary organization. These groups quickly disappeared, the product of FBI repression, the end of the Vietnam War, and their own ideological folly. European and American Communist parties that described their doctrine as "Marxist-Leninist" dissolved after the collapse of the Soviet Union in 1991.

Social Democracy: In 1896, Eduard Bernstein, a top leader of the SPD, took issue with his party's commitment to orthodox Marxism, rejecting the Marxist insistence that a revolutionary rupture, led by an immiserated blue-collar majority, would create socialism. Instead, Bernstein argued that the white collar and small-propertied middle classes would continue to grow along with the working class, and that both classes would thrive rather than suffer under a capitalist system that had learned to avoid crises. Socialism would eventually arrive through the ballot and legislature—through an accretion of reforms and through the gradual acceptance by capitalists themselves of socialist ethical ideals. Bernstein continued to embrace Marx's goal of socialism, but he declared, "This goal, whatever it may be, is nothing to me, the movement is everything."

Bernstein's great contribution was to attempt to ground socialist politics in the realities of capitalism—to recognize that the development of capitalism was not leading inexorably to a class struggle between a blue-collar proletariat and a white-collar bourgeoisie that would usher in an entirely new society and economy. But Bernstein was also wrong about capitalism having surmounted crises and about capitalists' eventual acceptance of socialism.

During his lifetime, Bernstein's comrades denounced him as a revisionist. But after World War II, the general thrust of his politics—with an addition of the economics of John Maynard Keynes—became the prevailing outlook of socialist parties, including the SPD. Even when party leaders have abjured any allegiance to socialism, the parties have remained nominally committed to democratic socialism, and factions within the parties have kept the flame alive. In Great Britain, for instance, Tony Blair's revision to the pro-socialist Clause IV of the Labour Party's constitution began nevertheless with the words, "The Labour Party is a democratic socialist party." But Bernstein's assignment of socialism to a distant, imperceptible future led some of these parties to accept the logic of market capitalism

26   and to acquiesce in policies that eliminated significant differ-
        ences between them and the parties of the center-right.

Post-Marxist Socialism

The leading socialist politicians in the United States and
the U.K. and the great majority of people who voted for them
do not endorse orthodox Marxism. And there is a group of
socialist theorists—many of them former orthodox Marxists—
who have tried to spell out the underlying assumptions of a
new socialism and socialist politics. They include economist
Thomas Piketty, philosophers Nancy Fraser and Axel Honneth, the late historian Martin J. Sklar, the late sociologist
Erik Wright, historian James Livingston, political scientists
Albena Azmanova, John D. Stephens, and Sheri Berman, and
sociologists Lane Kenworthy, Fred Block, Margaret Somers,
and Stephanie Mudge. One can find sharp disagreements
among them, even about the use of the word "socialism," but
on the basis of their work, one can see the beginnings of a new
post-Marxist, post–Cold War, post-industrial socialist politics that comports with, and draws out the assumptions of,
what today's socialist politicians and their voters are saying
and thinking. These are its key features:

Socialism within Capitalism: The new socialists reject Marx's
theory of punctuated stages of history as well as the social-
democratic view of socialism as the end point on an infinite
line. Instead, they see socialism as developing *within* capitalism,
the way capitalism developed within feudalism. Socialism creates institutions and laws that fulfill the ethical ideals of liberty,
equality, justice, democracy, and social solidarity.

Socialist economic institutions and programs can be developed within capitalism that shift economic and social power from capital ("the rich and powerful") toward labor ("working people"). Examples can include a stiff wealth tax that can be used to fund public programs or redistribute capital, "co-determination" laws that grant workers' representatives equal power on corporate boards, the creation of regulatory agencies to police corporate behavior, and public ownership and control of essential services or industries (such as healthcare, education, transportation, and energy production). In *Capital and Ideology,* Piketty describes a "participatory socialism" in which workers would serve on corporate boards and in which "a progressive tax on private wealth" would "diffuse wealth at the base while limiting concentration at the summit," such that the capitalist class would cease to be an inheritable caste.

In an essay, "The Capitalism-Socialism Mix," Martin J. Sklar contended that the competitive capitalism of Marx's days had been transformed into "a mix of public and private sectors as seats of authority and initiative in shaping, planning, regulating, and containing development, or, to put it in baldly ideological terms, the mix of socialism and capitalism." Sklar described twentieth-century American history as a symbiosis, and clash, between socialist and capitalist relations of production. In *The Idea of Socialism*, German philosopher Axel Honneth described "the social legislation of the early twentieth century (e.g., the law of co-determination in West Germany, minimum wages in various countries, etc.) not merely as contingent measures, but as the first steps of progress along the long and difficult path to the socialization of the labor market." Erik Wright wrote of socialist reforms and institutions,

28   including cooperatives, worker-owned business, and nonprofit businesses developing within the niches of capitalism and progressively expanding their reach:

> Alternative, noncapitalist economic activities, embodying democratic and egalitarian relations, emerge in the niches where possible within an economy dominated by capitalism . . . . Struggles involving the state take place, sometimes to protect these spaces, other times to facilitate new possibilities . . . . Eventually, the cumulative effect of this interplay between changes from above and initiatives from below may reach a point where the socialist relations created within the economic ecosystem become sufficiently prominent in the lives of individuals and communities that capitalism can no longer be said to be dominant.

In other words, the mix of capitalism and socialism would change in favor of socialism. Sociologist Fred Block, citing Polanyi's view of socialism as "the subordination of markets to democratic politics," contends that "there is no single moment of transition from a profit-oriented economy to a socialist economy; it is rather an evolutionary process through which there is an ever greater and deeper extension of democracy into economic decisionmaking."

Socialism as a Just System: Marx and many orthodox Marxists and Marxist-Leninists have tended to play down the ethical appeal of socialism. While Marx thundered against capitalist injustice in his political writings, he didn't believe moral considerations, but only economic exploitation, would drive the

transition to socialism. The German philosopher Karl Volander
recalled in 1904, "The moment anyone started to talk to Marx
about morality, he would roar with laughter." But the new
socialists, echoing the concerns of Christian and ethical socialists, place a high importance on the ideals of justice as integral
to socialism.

The philosopher G.A. Cohen, whose initial work parroted
orthodox Marxism, argued for the ethical appeal of community and equality in his last book, *Why Not Socialism?* Cohen
describes a camping trip, where, typically, everyone is expected
to do their share of the work, and where the goods are held in
common and shared. "It is commonly true on camping trips," he
writes, "that people cooperate within a common concern that,
so far as is possible, everybody has a roughly similar opportunity to flourish." Cohen envisaged socialism as the attempt to
extend the camping trip's "socialist way with collective property
and mutual giving" to parts of a capitalism, such as healthcare.

The new socialists also don't limit their effort to obtain justice to the workplace. In the wake of the feminist and civil rights
movements, they want, in Nancy Fraser's words, to "overcome
domination across the board, in society as well as the economy."
They don't believe that ending economic exploitation will have
a cascading effect on all other forms of domination, but believe
that socialist reforms and institutions have to be measured by a
broader yardstick that includes racial and sexual equality.

The Primacy of Politics: The new socialists reject Marx's historical determinism—his view that growing crises would lead
inexorably to socialism—as well as Bernstein's optimistic
view that growing prosperity would convince citizens from all

30   classes of the desirability of the socialist ideal. Many of them, including Piketty, Berman, Fraser, Block, and Somers, were heavily influenced by Polanyi's masterwork, *The Great Transformation*, which appeared in 1944. Polanyi described a "double movement" at the center of capitalism—an oscillating struggle that has pitted a dystopian ideal of laissez-faire capitalism—in which workers, deprived of social protection, are at the mercy of the private labor market—against the attempt by the working and allied classes to erect fortifications against their isolation and exploitation.

New socialists see continual clashes between those who favor one or the other side of Polanyi's double movement. In American and European history, capitalism has gone through different eras that have been defined by which of these forces reigned supreme. In the United States, for instance, the period from 1932 to 1972 saw the erection of extensive social protections against corporate capitalism and, after World War II, internationally against the rigidity of the gold standard. In 1980, after a decade of turbulence caused by economic downturns, an energy crisis, and rising international competition, the U.S. and Great Britain both entered a period where what Block and Somers call "market fundamentalism" held sway domestically and internationally.

During this recent period, socialist institutions within capitalism were dismantled or gutted. In the United States, for instance, government agencies meant to encourage unionization, regulate finance, and protect consumers and the environment were captured by those businesses they were mandated to regulate. In the wake of the Great Recession and the depression caused by the global coronavirus pandemic, the U.S. and

Europe appear to be entering a new period in which it is likely that forces favoring social protection will hold sway. But it's not clear what political form that protection will take. It is by no means certain that it will be socialist.

In the 1930s, as Polanyi noted in *The Great Transformation*, both Roosevelt's New Deal (which he saw as a kind of proto-socialism) and Hitler's Nazism were reactions to economic collapse. Both offered extensive social protections. But in Hitler's case, he did so by eliminating democracy and scapegoating and murdering Jews and others deemed undesirable. Similarly, today, the breakdown of the economy during the Great Recession and the coronavirus pandemic could lead to authoritarian and even neo-fascist governments as well as democratic socialist ones. As Sheri Berman argues in *The Primacy of Politics*, what happens will depend on politics, not on inexorable historical laws.

Explicit and Implicit Socialism: To understand that socialism can develop within capitalism is to concede that socialist reforms and institutions have not necessarily been and will not necessarily be introduced in the name of socialism. Some notable institutions, such as Britain's National Health Service or Germany's co-determination law, were spurred by socialist parties. So was Francois Mitterrand's ill-fated enactment of the Common Program in 1981 or the Swedish Social Democrats' Meidner Plan, which would have given stock in corporations to workers. But in the United States, the New Deal and the reforms enacted during the Johnson administration, which shifted the balance of power from capital to labor, were not seen as "socialist"— except, perhaps, by conservative opponents.

There are two kinds of circumstances where this can take place. The first is when the word "socialism" has become so stigmatized that proponents of a reform hesitate to use it. That has certainly been the case in the United States during the Cold War era and remains so for many Americans born before 1980. In the 2020 Democratic primaries, Massachusetts senator Elizabeth Warren championed institutional reforms that were identical to those proposed by Sanders—for instance, putting workers on corporate boards and giving them stock. But she insisted she was a "capitalist to the bone."

The second, and more peculiar, circumstance is when a socialist reform is championed by politicians and parties that in other respects are overtly hostile to socialism and friendly to free-market capitalism. Many of America's most powerful regulatory agencies, including the Environmental Protection Agency and the Occupational Safety and Health Administration, were signed into law during the first term of the Republican Nixon administration. These reforms came from pressure from below, but they were supported by the administration. Currently in Europe, the Greens, which have often been friendly to free-market capitalism, have begun to support programs that would enhance public control of energy production.

In his last book, *How to be an Anti-Capitalist in the 21st Century*, posthumously published in 2019, Erik Olin Wright warned that "perhaps the word 'socialism' itself should be dropped. Words accumulate meaning through historical contexts, and maybe socialism has been so compromised by its association with twentieth-century repressive regimes that it can no longer serve well as the umbrella term for emancipatory alternatives to capitalism." But he added that "in the first decade of the twenty-first century, the idea of socialism has regained some of its positive moral standing."

Populist Politics: The new socialists also reject the political scenario advanced by orthodox Marxists. They do not regard the industrial working class as the vanguard of a socialist revolution. In the 1985 book *Hegemony and Socialist Strategy*, which became the ur-text of post-Marxism, political theorists Ernesto Laclau and Chantal Mouffe wrote:

> What is now in crisis is a whole conception of socialism which rests upon the ontological centrality of the working class, upon the role of Revolution with a capital "r," as the founding moment in the transition of one type of society to another, and upon the illusory prospect of a perfectly unitary and homogeneous collective will that will render pointless the moment of politics.

Bernstein foresaw that the industrial working class would stop growing as a percentage of the labor force. But he mistakenly believed that it would be crowded out by the growth of a property-owning middle class. Instead, what has evolved is a waged and salaried labor force that is diverse (white and blue collar) and highly stratified in income, status, and authority, as well as often divided politically by race, nationality, and culture. It ranges from day-laborers to unionized college professors. It does not own the means of production, but it does not inherently see itself as a single exploited class, either. Indeed,

34 segments of it are often at odds politically. If it is to be united, it will have to be through the medium of politics and not simply through metronomic appeals to "the working class."

In their book, Laclau and Mouffe recommend Italian revolutionary Antonio Gramsci's idea of a "historic bloc," but while that term has some explanatory power, it is unwieldy as a public rallying cry. ("Members of the historic bloc, unite!") Laclau and Mouffe would later embrace the populist use of the term "people," and in the last decades, socialists in the United States, Britain, Spain, Greece, and France have framed their appeals through political logic of populism, pitting "the people," "the working people," or "working families" against an "establishment" or "elite." Sanders sometimes will talk of the working class, but when he does, he invariably includes people like teachers and nurses who would not have qualified under orthodox Marxist criteria.

The Socialist Appeal

Most of the new socialists were writing in the 1990s and early 2000s, when market fundamentalism still prevailed in the U.S. and Europe. They were more advocating rather than describing a socialist politics. The economies of the United States and Europe were in decent shape, so their appeal was almost entirely moral. In 1994, the British philosopher G.A. Cohen, acknowledging that a homogeneous working class could no longer be counted on to lead the revolution, appealed to socialist values as the means to unite a majority. "The moral force of those values never depended on the social force supporting them that is now disappearing," he wrote. In his last book, *Justice as Fairness: A Restatement,* published in 2001, the moral philosopher John

Rawls embraced a version of democratic socialism as best satis-
fying his criteria for a just society.

A moral appeal, based on the Sermon on the Mount and the egalitarian ideals of the American and French revolutions, was central to the rise of socialism. It was compromised by revolutions in the Soviet Union, China, and the "Third World" that in the name of socialism rejected liberty and democracy, but has revived since the collapse of the Soviet Union. It informs socialists' rejection of economic inequality and of racial, sexual, and ethnic discrimination. During the last decade, these appeals have been highlighted by the anger at the power of a "billionaire class," of which Trump is a glaring example, and by the protests against police brutality toward African Americans, which have spread well beyond the black community.

But the Great Recession and the looming danger of climate change, followed by the pandemic depression, have provided a set of material grievances about capitalism and an interest in socialism. Like the Great Depression of the 1930s, the pandemic depression could potentially unite the middle and bottom of society against the heights of power and wealth in a quest for economic security and justice. The principal obstacle, as in the past, will be a politics that uses sociocultural appeals to break up the left's historic constituency. This tactic is traditionally employed by the political right, but it can also be introduced unwittingly by liberals and the left when they subordinate potentially unifying economic concerns to radical strictures over race, nationality, and gender that go beyond democratic rights.

The key figure in matching the ideals of socialism with the material grievances of the present has been Sanders. He

36 more than anyone gave voice and prominence to democratic socialism. His own political career is testimony to the transition from orthodox Marxism to a new political philosophy that sees socialism developing within capitalism and that adopts the political logic of populism rather than of traditional Marxist socialism. Inevitably, even Sanders will fade from the scene (his counterpart in Britain, Jeremy Corbyn, already has), but they helped inspire young people in the United States and Great Britain to embrace a new socialist politics.

Whether a socialist politics becomes a significant alternative to an accommodating liberalism or conservatism depends on whether new generations of politicians and political organizations can marshal the growing dissatisfaction with capitalism into a viable politics. That in turn depends on at least two things. First, they must avoid eschatological fantasies in favor of a vision of socialism that appears to be viable and feasible. Second, they should seek a common ground in economic grievance and democratic aspiration and avoid potentially divisive extreme sociocultural appeals that go beyond the ideas that informed socialism. These would include, for instance, contemporary opposition not simply to discrimination based on adopted genders, but any distinctions based upon gender, or support not simply for comprehensive immigration reform, but for no limits at all on immigration.

That socialists can avoid these pitfalls is by no means certain. In the U.K., Corbyn and the young socialists in Momentum succeeded to some extent in formulating a viable socialism, but failed to unite Labour's traditional downscale constituencies with its growing support among young people in London and in university towns. In the United States, which lacks the

equivalent of an even nominally socialist or social-democratic
party, socialist politics is at a more rudimentary level, but the
anti-capitalist sentiment and public sympathy for socialism
is growing from one generation to the next. The question is
whether this sentiment can become the basis for a formidable political movement. Besides Sanders and Ocasio-Cortez,
there are no national politicians right now that can shape a
post-Marxist socialist politics. DSA, while growing, is still a
relatively small group that lacks a national presence. While the
organization as a whole reflects the influence of Sanders's politics, the group's activist core also contains zealous orthodox
Marxists and adherents of identity politics that could condemn
it to irrelevance. Like Momentum, its politics often reflects
the parochial sociocultural preoccupations of the big post-
industrial cities and university towns.

More promising, perhaps, is the development of politicians
and political organizations that, while not explicitly socialist,
have adopted programs and policies that would achieve some
measure of socialism within capitalism. That was certainly the
case with Warren in the Democratic presidential race, and there
are scores now of senators and House members who share her
and Sanders's views on the need to change the balance of power
and wealth in America. There are also many leftwing organizations that have adopted at least part of a socialist agenda, but
they, too, shy away from the language of socialism. In a decade,
these politicians and organizations and their successors may
come to believe that an appeal to democratic socialism best
captures the need to dramatically reform capitalism. Or, perhaps, socialism will appear, as Erik Wright suggests, under an
assumed name.

American Socialism from Debs to Sanders

The two great figures in the history of American socialism are Eugene V. Debs and Bernie Sanders. Debs led the American Socialist Party during the early part of the twentieth century when it had some influence—enough certainly to strike fear in the hearts of American business leaders who were deathly afraid of what was called "class politics." Sanders has been responsible more than anyone for bringing a discussion of democratic socialism back into American politics.

Sanders traces his politics back to Debs. In 1979, he wrote and acted in a half-hour documentary celebrating Debs as "the greatest leader in the history of the American working class." With his thick Brooklyn accent, Sanders, who could not afford to hire a professional actor, recited Debs's injunction to "vote for the Socialist Party because it is the only party unequivocally committed to the abolition of the wage system." Sanders has a plaque of Debs in his senate office and continues to carry Debs's key chain in his pocket as a political talisman.

Journalists and historians today also draw the connection between the two men. In *USA Today*, Jonathan Turley described Sanders as Debs's "obvious political successor." In the *New Yorker*, historian Jill Lepore describes Sanders carrying Debs's socialism "into the twenty-first century." And there certainly are respects in which Sanders has patterned himself after Debs. Like Debs, Sanders has refused to embrace what Debs called the "Democratic or Republican machine of capitalism." And like Debs, Sanders has thundered against what Debs called the "privileged class." But in understanding today's politics, the differences between the two men are more important than the similarities.

If you look at Debs's career, and the evolution of his political beliefs, he went from heading a business-friendly craft union to being an exponent of orthodox Marxist socialism, with some American variations. Sanders, on the other hand, went from being an orthodox Marxist to a congressman, senator, and presidential candidate who espouses something like the new socialism of Wright, Block, or Piketty. The two men's political journeys almost go in reverse.

From Owen to Debs

The first wave of socialist advocacy in the United States came during the first half of the nineteenth century and was inspired by the beginning of a factory system, which threatened the Jeffersonian promise of a classless democracy. There were hundreds of utopian communities established, including Robert Owen's New Harmony in Indiana and the Transcendentalists' Brook Farm outside of Boston. Most of these failed to survive

40   the Civil War. Owen's attempt in 1825 to create a "community of equality" lasted only two years. The second wave came with the rapid industrialization that took place in the last three decades of the nineteenth century, which was accompanied by financial panics, economic downturns, the rise of the Populists, and the growth of a labor movement.

Like the utopians, the socialists of the late nineteenth century were intellectuals who condemned industrialization as a violation of America's founding principles and Christian ethics. George Herron, a Congregationalist minister, castigated capitalist competition as "the mark of Cain." "The day is coming," said Herron, "in which a truly Christian social order would exist on earth, the fulfillment in the here and now of God's Kingdom of Heaven." In 1888, Edward Bellamy, the son of a minister, published *Looking Backward*, which became an international bestseller. It foresaw an America of 2000 in which industry was nationalized, incomes were equal, and workers retired at age forty-five. Bellamy inspired 127 Nationalist Clubs to be established, but they disbanded after Bellamy decided to back the Peoples' Party in 1892. One small and irrelevant Marxist socialist group, the Socialist Labor Party, was founded in 1876. Composed primarily of recent immigrants from Central Europe, it initially conducted its meetings in German.

What finally spurred the formation of a socialist movement and party was labor unrest, which was heightened by the depression of the 1890s, when unemployment rose to over 12 percent, wages were cut, and many families, lacking the later benefits of a welfare state, found themselves in desperate straits. When the steelworkers, rail workers, and miners went out on strike, the states and federal government helped put down the strikes with force. In 1894, thirty-four American Railway Union strikers were killed. Debs, the leader of the American Railway Union, who had earlier condemned strikes and called for a harmonious relationship between workers and employers, was radicalized by the experience.

Eugene Victor Debs was born in 1855 in Terre Haute, Indiana, which had been a center of the Methodist Second Great Awakening. Debs was not observant, but his understanding of politics and socialism was shaped by the prevalent social gospel. "What is socialism? Merely Christianity in action. It recognizes the equality in men," he wrote in 1898, the year he declared himself a socialist. Debs had worked as a locomotive fireman as a teenager and had become an official of the Brotherhood of Locomotive Firemen, which functioned as a benevolent society. The young Debs was by no means a socialist. "My view of capital and labor is that a community should exist between the capitalist and the laborer, instead of antagonistic feelings," he declared. Debs opposed the great railroad strike of 1877.

But a succession of strikes provoked by wage cuts during downturns, and paralyzing jurisdictional disputes during the strikes between railway unions, where the conductors refused to support the firemen and engineers, convinced Debs in 1893 to create a single railway union. The American Railway Union won its first strike but was destroyed during the Pullman strike the next year. Debs and other strike leaders were sent to prison. Jailed in a house in Woodstock, Illinois, Debs read Bellamy, Laurence Gronlund (the author of *The Cooperative Commonwealth*, a popularization of Marx), Marx's *Capital*, George Herron, and Kautsky. Debs recalled being most influenced by Kautsky's *The Class Struggle*, which had become the standard exposition of

42   orthodox Marxism. The book, Debs wrote later, had helped him "out of darkness into light."

Debs did not immediately embrace Marxist socialism. In 1897, he tried to set up utopian colonies where laborers could "work out their own salvation, their redemption, and independence." But in June of the next year, he and Victor Berger, a Milwaukee socialist who was acting at that point as Debs's mentor in socialist politics, established the Social Democratic Party, and Debs ran for president as the party's nominee in 1900. A year later, the party was rechristened the Socialist Party. Debs would run again for president in 1904, 1908, 1912, and in 1920 when he was imprisoned in Atlanta for "sedition" because of his opposition to American entry into World War I.

There were elements of the Socialist Party and of Debs's socialism that were peculiar to America of the early twentieth century. The party had some support among trade unionists in the East and Midwest, but a third of its members came from west of the Mississippi, and many of these socialists were former Populists who were part of the region's farm economy. Many were driven by a simple hatred of Wall Street and big business. In these areas and in the Midwest, the Protestant social gospel informed the party's socialist appeal. Its meetings, held in campgrounds and sometimes in buildings that also served as churches, were like revivals. After visiting socialists in Oklahoma, journalist Oscar Ameringer remarked, "They took their socialism like a new religion."

Debs, a stem-winding, thundering orator who spoke to crowds before there were microphones, framed his own appeal for socialism in Christian terms. "The workers are the saviors of society; the redeemers of the race," Debs declared. Jesus was the

"master proletarian revolutionist and sower of the social whirl-
wind," Debs wrote. But his Christianity reinforced, and col-
ored, an orthodox Marxism that he had learned from Kautsky.
Socialism ("when the bells peal forth the joyous tidings") was
a new stage of history that would inevitably be ushered in by a
revolution that would occur when the working class, suffering
from immiseration, overthrew the capitalists.

In his acceptance speech in 1912 for the presidential nomination, Debs described a society "divided into two classes—
capitalists and workers, exploiters and producers." Even though
the American economy had grown about 4 percent a year since
the end of the 1890s depression, Debs invoked the dialectic of
immiseration. "So long as the nation's resources and productive and distributive machinery are the private property of a
privileged class, the masses will be at their mercy, poverty will
be their lot, and life will be shorn of all that raises it above the
brute level."

The Socialist Party, Debs insisted, would not cooperate
to pursue immediate reforms with the two capitalist parties
(three in 1912, with Theodore Roosevelt's Progressive Party) or
with Samuel Gompers's American Federation of Labor, which
opposed Debs's socialism. "It is vain to hope for material relief
upon the prevailing system of capitalism," he declared. "All the
reforms that are proposed by the three capitalist parties, even
if carried out in good faith, would still leave the working class
in industrial slavery." Workers' only alternative was to vote for
"emancipation" by supporting socialism and the Socialist Party.

Under Debs's leadership, the Socialist Party grew. In 1901,
it had 10,000 members; by 1912, it had 118,000. It elected 1,200
public officials and published over 300 periodicals. Its main

44 publication, the Kansas-based *Appeal to Reason*, had a circulation of almost a million. In the 1912 election, Debs garnered 901,551 votes, or 6 percent of the total. Party leaders looked forward to the Socialists doubling their membership by the next election, but the 1912 election was to prove the party's high-water mark.

In 1919, the party split over its response to the Russian Revolution of 1917, and over the call by the Soviets to engage in armed revolution. A new Communist Party attracted many of the party's foreign-language federations, which by the decade's end made up half of its membership. By 1929, the party had shrunk to 6,000 registered members, and few were active. It revived briefly under ex-minister Norman Thomas's leadership, but never came close to regaining even the very modest influence it had enjoyed early in the century.

Why did the Socialist Party fail to gain a foothold in American politics? There is a century-long debate that began with Werner Sombart's 1906 treatise, *Why Is There No Socialism in the United States*? But there are really two different questions involved, although the answers are related. First, why did the Socialist Party fail? Second, why did socialism fail to win adherents?

The first question is easy to answer. In a two-party system, a third party can only break through if it stands for something that the other two parties are against or are indifferent toward, *and* if what it stands for has a significant public appeal—enough, for instance, to win states in the electoral college. The Republican Party that was founded in 1854 opposed the extension of slavery in the West that the Democrats and Whigs wouldn't halt; in

1968, George Wallace and his American Independent Party opposed racial desegregation that both major parties favored. The Socialist Party espoused a cause—socialism—that neither the Republicans nor the Democrats supported, but socialism did not command a huge following in America. And by 1912, progressive Republicans or liberal Democrats were addressing issues like unemployment compensation that immediately concerned the workers the Socialists wanted to attract.

The second question of why socialism never attracted a large following is more difficult. Sombart himself cited the American workers' rising standard of living. That was certainly a factor, although not in the Great Depression. Also important was Americans' default suspicion of "big government," which goes back to the revolution of 1776, and made Americans suspicious of a politics that seemed to promise an overweening government. And then, of course, was the popular identification of socialism with Soviet communism, which during the Cold War subverted discussions even of democratic socialism. (The American Communist Party never had a significant public following. In 1932, its presidential candidate received 0.26 percent of the vote. It had its greatest success during the Popular Front period from 1935 to 1945 when its operatives concealed their ultimate objectives and often their membership in the party.)

Perhaps the most important reason of all, as sociologist Daniel Bell argued in *Marxian Socialism in the United States*, is that Debs's and the Socialist Party's conception of socialism was otherworldly. Echoing Lowith's analysis of Marxism, Bell noted the "religious chiliastic origin of modern socialism." "Socialism is an eschatological movement; it is sure of its destiny because

46 'history' leads to its goal," Bell wrote. Socialism was the second coming, the establishment of the Kingdom of God on Earth.

Debs' Socialist Party was not a religious movement as such, but it had significant elements of one. Religious movements seek converts, not voters. The lure of a religious movement is precisely its otherworldliness—its promise of redemption and salvation beyond the woes of present life. Politics, on the other hand, seeks majorities that will allow politicians to address present hopes and grievances, such as (in Debs's era) the prevalence of child labor, the absence of a minimum wage, the lack of unemployment compensation, the frequency of farm foreclosures, and the use of the courts and of state or federal troops against strikers. Debs's and the Socialists' popularity was based initially on some voters' belief that neither of the major parties were addressing these immediate issues and that they could only be addressed as a result of socialist revolution, which would totally transform society. Politics and religion were fused, as they were for Christian socialists like George Herron. But as soon as the major parties did begin to address those immediate issues, voters abandoned socialism's otherworldly appeal

If apocalyptical socialism's lack of appeal wasn't obvious in Debs's time, it became obvious in 1932 when ordained minister Norman Thomas ran for president against Franklin Roosevelt on a platform claiming that only socialism could cure America's ills. Despite being an effective orator who could appeal to moral and religious stirrings, Thomas received 2 percent of the vote. Many of the labor activists and officials who had remained in the Socialist Party quit afterward, and the party itself became a playground for followers of the exiled Leon Trotsky. These followers of Trotsky, believing that Russia's Bolsheviks had

succeeded because of their "correct line" rather than their numbers, repeatedly divided themselves when faced with current
political questions into further factions and parties, each of
which claimed to be more correct than the others.

Victor Berger and Socialism in Our Time

Victor Berger and the Milwaukee Socialists are the exception
that proved the rule—that it was Debs's conception of socialism
and socialist politics that doomed the party. Debs was a centrist
figure within the party, while Berger was squarely on the right.
Berger, who immigrated to the United States from Austria at age
eighteen, had been an orthodox Marxist, but in 1901, he read
and was deeply impressed by Bernstein's *Evolutionary Socialism*.

Berger, who was editing German- and English-language
newspapers, built the Milwaukee branch of the Socialist Party
around the idea that by winning immediate improvements for
the city's working and middle class, such as the creation of a
municipal water system or a minimum wage, the party would
be creating the rudiments of socialism within capitalism. "In
that way," he wrote, "we can have a great deal of 'Socialism in our
Time' even though we cannot have the full-fledged Cooperative Commonwealth." Berger's socialism would also not exclude
private property and ownership. "Everything the individual can
own and manage best, the individual is to own and manage," he
wrote. Berger did believe in the end goal of socialism, but cau-
tioned that it would take "another century or two" and occur
through a peaceful transition.

Berger was not Debs's match as a moral exemplar. He was a
racist who supported the American Federation of Labor's exclu-
sion of blacks. But he created an effective political machine in

48   Milwaukee that held power in the city with few interruptions from 1910 to 1960, and he was elected to the House four times. As one of only two Socialists in Congress, Berger worked, when appropriate, with progressive Democrats and Republicans on legislation. In Milwaukee, the Socialists stood for good government against a corrupt Democratic Party and a weak Republican Party. The Milwaukee Socialist Party's creation of a water and sanitation system earned it the sobriquet "sewer socialism" and "showcialists" from leftwing critics contemptuous of reforms that merely "patched up" capitalism without creating bell-ringing socialism.

Berger's achievement in Milwaukee could not necessarily have been replicated nationally—certainly not in the 1930s, when Roosevelt and the New Deal advanced the same kinds of reforms within capitalism that Berger had advocated. And from 1917 to 1989, the Soviet claim to socialism cast a shadow in America over any attempt to win support for any policy openly tied to "socialism." But if Sanders is linked to the past, it is not to Debs but to Berger. Berger's "Socialism in our Time" is the bridge to Sanders and the socialist awakening of the 2010s.

Sanders and the New Left

Sanders, who was born in Brooklyn in 1941 to working-class immigrants, was a participant in the beginnings of what C. Wright Mills in 1960 called the "new left." The new left, unlike the left of the 1890s or 1930s, was not primarily inspired by economic privation—the sixties were a boom time for the country—but by the rise of the civil rights movement, the movement for nuclear disarmament, and, after 1964, the movement against the Vietnam War. In 1961, Sanders transferred

from Brooklyn College to the University of Chicago, which was
an incubator of the new left.

At the University of Chicago, Sanders became a member of CORE, the civil rights group that was trying to desegregate the housing that the university owned. He also joined the Young People's Socialist League (YPSL), the youth branch of what remained of the Socialist Party. The national party was dominated by the writer Michael Harrington and his proponents, who were in favor of working within the Democratic Party to realign it. (Harrington would go on to found the Democratic Socialists of America in 1982.) But the Chicago chapter included Joel Geier and Mike Parker, who wanted to create a new labor party.

After graduation, Sanders spent six months on a Kibbutz in Israel, then relocated to New York City, and finally, in 1970, he moved permanently to Vermont. In moving to Vermont, Sanders embraced a very different strain of the new left— the counter-culture. The "beatniks" of the 1950s had been an avant-garde artistic movement; the "hippies" of the 1960s counter-culture were a social movement that embraced sex, drugs, and rock 'n' roll. The counter-culture also had its political prophets who espoused a version of utopian socialism. One of these was Bronx-born Vermonter Murray Bookchin, an anarchist who despised the Marxist-Leninist groupuscules that arose out of the new left in the late 1960s and advocated instead the spread of "libertarian municipalities." In 1981, when Sanders first became a U.S. Congressman in 1991, Bookchin's daughter Debbie would become his first press secretary.

By 1970, Vermont had become a center for back-to-the-land hippies. It was dotted with communes. One writer

50 estimated in 1970 that there were 35,800 hippies in Vermont, comprising one-third of the state's residents between the ages of eighteen and thirty-four. Sanders's shack in Stannard was near Earth Peoples' Park, Quarry Hill, and New Hamburger Commune. Sanders was of a slightly earlier generation—he was not big on drugs or rock 'n' roll—but he integrated his opposition to the Vietnam War and his vision of socialism with the preoccupations of the counter-culture. In the *Freeman*, an alternative newspaper, Sanders attacked the American intervention in Vietnam and "a United States Congress composed of millionaires and state legislatures controlled by lobbyists." But Sanders, the newly minted utopian socialist, also assured his readers:

> The Revolution is coming, and it is a very beautiful revolution. . . . What is most important in this revolution will require no guns, no commandants, no screaming "leaders," and no vicious publications accusing everyone else of being counterrevolutionary. The revolution comes when two strangers smile at each other, when a father refuses to send his child to school because schools destroy children, when a commune is started and people begin to trust each other, when a young man refuses to go to war, and when a girl pushes aside all that her mother has "taught" her and accepts her boyfriend's love.

Sanders first ran for office in a 1972 special election as the Senate candidate of the newly formed Liberty Union, a third party dedicated to ending "the war in Vietnam, the militarization of society, the problems of the poor, and destruction of the environment." But in this election, and during his run for governor in November, Sanders also called for the abolition of "all

laws dealing with abortion, drugs, sexual behavior (homosexu-
ality, adultery etc.)," widening highway on-ramps to interstate
highways to enable hitchhiking, and ending "compulsory education." And Sanders campaigned as a socialist. "I even mentioned
the horrible word 'socialism'—and nobody in the audience
fainted," Sanders wrote in a campaign diary of his gubernato-
rial race.

Over the next four years, Sanders would run once more for
Senate and once more for governor. As the economic boom of
the 1960s ended with a sharp recession and an energy crisis,
Sanders became focused more on economic issues. Sanders
claimed he found support for nationalizing banks. "We talked to
working people and we got through to working people," he said.
"If you say that we have to take over the banks and have a substantial number of people vote for that position, that idea suddenly becomes acceptable reality."

Sanders had received only 2 percent of the vote in his first
election, and 1 percent in his second, but in his 1976 gubernato-
rial run he picked up 6.1 percent, enough to qualify the Liberty
Union for an ongoing spot on the ballot. The next year, however,
Sanders quit the Liberty Union, complaining that the party had
become "dormant."

In 1981, at the urging of Richard Sugarman, a philosophy
professor and friend, Sanders decided to run for mayor of Burlington, but Sugarman warned Sanders not to make the election about his socialist ideology. "No one gives a damn about
your ideology," Sugarman recalls telling Sanders. Sanders ran on
a platform of opposing condominiums on Burlington's waterfront and a property tax increase and promising to recruit a
minor league baseball team and to open a hill for sledding during

52   the winter. He rarely used the word "socialist." He won by ten votes against a Democratic incumbent.

Sanders's tenure as mayor recalled that of the Milwaukee Socialists. Speaking to the *Burlington Free Press* the next year, he described "one of his major priorities" was "to take the city from what was a very inefficient government and to make it into a modern corporation." And he succeeded in eliminating cronyism and balancing the city's books. Over the next eight years, he created affordable housing, initiated rent controls, established a land trust to fund housing purchases by low-income Vermonters, turned Burlington's unsightly waterfront into a park, and revitalized the city's downtown. He even got the Cincinnati Reds to start a farm team in Burlington. In 1987, *U.S. News and World Report* chose him as one of America's top twenty mayors.

During that time, Sanders didn't conceal that he was a socialist. A Debs election poster hung in the mayor's office. He described himself to writer Russell Banks as a "Eugene V. Debs type of socialist." *Rolling Stone* called him "the red mayor in the green mountains."

But Sanders didn't draw a direct connection between being a socialist and what he did as mayor. He told a reporter from the *Baltimore Sun*, "We acknowledge very frankly our limitations. If you ask me if the banks should be nationalized, I would say yes. But I don't have the power to nationalize the banks in Burlington." He organized a Progressive (not a socialist) Coalition in Burlington that backed his policies and ran candidates for city council.

When he ran for Vermont's one congressional seat in 1988, he did run as a Debs socialist. When asked by the *Rutland Daily Herald* about socialism, he said, "I'm not afraid of government control in economics. And I'm not afraid of government control in major enterprises if need be." Attacked as a potential spoiler by Democrats, he countered that a victory for him would lay the groundwork for a leftwing third party in the country. Sanders lost by 8,911 votes to Republican Peter Smith.

In June 1989, after he had left his job as mayor, Sanders sounded the tocsin for a socialist third party. Speaking before the National Committee for Independent Political Action in New York, Sanders declared that "it is absolutely imperative that we build an independent, democratic socialist left which has the guts to raise the issues that all of us know to be true, but which are rarely even *discussed* within establishment politics." He was still following Debs's lead. A year later, however, he no longer was.

Swedish-Style Socialist

In his 1990 rematch with Smith, Sanders ran as an independent but no longer proposed building a new socialist party. Instead, he promised, if elected, to caucus with the Democrats. In response, the Democrats ran only a token opponent against him and Smith. Sanders also abandoned his orthodox Marxist view of socialism. Instead, he styled himself a "Swedish-style socialist." As the *Burlington Free Press* reported, "Sanders says he supports democratic socialism as it exists in countries such as Sweden, where national healthcare and free college education are available."

Asked to define his kind of socialism, Sanders told the *Rutland Daily Herald*, "When I talk about democratic socialism, what I am talking about is a style of government which has existed on and off in Scandinavia, Austria, England, West Germany, and

54 Canada." After Sanders was elected, he told the Associated Press, "All that socialism means to me is democracy with a small 'd.' To me, socialism doesn't mean state ownership of everything, by any means. It means creating a nation and a world in which all human beings have a decent standard of living."

What had happened? Sanders clearly became convinced that he could not be elected in Vermont or function in Congress as the candidate of a Debsian socialist party. But there were two other factors that swayed him, both of which were affirmed by someone who has worked in Sanders's office and his campaigns. First, Sanders's model of socialism had combined democracy with nationalization and a planned economy. When Sanders visited the Soviet Union in June 1988, he told reporters that Soviet officials hoped that through *perestroika* and *glasnost*, "democracy and socialism can exist in a compatible way." That seems to have been Sanders's hope as well, but the idea of socialism as a command economy of nationalized firms was dashed by the collapse of the Soviet Union.

Secondly, as a viable congressional candidate, Sanders had to confront the limits of what was possible at a time when the reforms of the New Deal, the Great Society, and even the Nixon years were under assault. He realized, the former aide said, that "there is only so much you can do in Congress."

By then, the Democratic Socialists of America, or the DSA, had been in existence for almost a decade. At a conference in 1991, Sanders was asked by a small group of DSA members whether he believed that a capitalist society needed to be replaced with a socialist society. After declaring that he was a democratic socialist, Sanders responded, "At this point in

American history, I would be very delighted if we could move in
a conservative manner in the direction of a country like Sweden,
which has a national healthcare system which guarantees free
healthcare, which has free education for all its kids."

Sanders had traveled within a year from Debs's orthodox
Marxism to a politics very similar to that of the Milwaukee
Socialists. Socialist politics were no longer an all-or-nothing
matter where you favored certain immediate reforms, but what
really counted was replacing capitalism *in toto*. Socialist politics consisted of seeking reforms that freed Americans from
capitalist market constraints in obtaining healthcare or a college education, or that enhanced the power of workers in their
workplace or business. Sanders told the DSA, "I think what you
are ultimately moving toward is partnerships. You are talking
about democratic control of the economy, you are talking about
a partnership between the private sector, the unions, the government, the working people." That's *not* public ownership and
control of the means of production; but it would mean a significant increase in the power of workers to control their destiny.
For Sanders, that represented a momentous shift in his outlook
and it opened the way for a reappraisal in American politics of
what socialism meant.

Socialism and the New Deal

As a member of the House starting in 1990 and then Senate from
2006, Sanders repeatedly put forth bills and amendments and
took votes that reflected his democratic socialism. In a different
era, perhaps, Sanders might have had considerable success with
his initiatives. But at a time when Republicans were committed

56   to market fundamentalism and the Democratic leadership was trying to envision a "third way"—that is, between New Deal liberalism and the Republican priorities—many of Sanders's positions put him at odds even with members of the Democratic Caucus. Sanders got few bills or amendments passed and became known as a gadfly and an outsider.

Sanders opposed a succession of "free trade" treaties, including the North American Free Trade Agreement and the granting of "most-favored-nation" trading status to China, on the grounds that they would threaten American jobs by encouraging corporations to move out of the country or allow low-wage foreign competitors to put American firms out of business. He proposed a Workplace Democracy Act that would make it easier for workers to form unions, repeal right-to-work laws, and widen the definition of employee protections under the National Labor Relations Board. He convinced only two other House members to sponsor the bill. Sanders began proposing a single-payer healthcare plan in 1993, in contrast to the Clinton plan for "managed care." In 2007, he unveiled a plan to encourage employee ownership and cooperatives. In 2010, he staged an eight-and-a-half-hour filibuster against a bill negotiated by the Obama administration with Republicans that perpetuated Bush-era tax cuts for the wealthy.

Many of Sanders's legislative initiatives—including his version of single-payer health insurance, dubbed Medicare for All, and a $15 minimum wage—became central to his presidential campaigns in 2016 and 2020. In October 2019, Sanders introduced a Corporate Accountability and Democracy Plan that would guarantee workers' representatives 45 percent of the members on corporate boards and gradually increase workers'

stock ownership until it reached 20 percent of the company.
Sanders's plan would, he claimed, "fundamentally shift the
wealth of the economy back into the hands of the workers who
create it," and "give workers an ownership stake in the companies they work for." These proposals went beyond what was then
seen as garden-variety "liberalism" or "progressivism." They
reflected an attempt to establish socialism within capitalism.

Sanders was criticized by prominent Democrats like Congressman Barney Frank because he "never got anything done,"
but Sanders attributed his failure to a Washington politics controlled by large donors and corporate lobbyists. In 2014, as he
pondered whether to run for president, he told Vox, "The major
political, strategic difference I have with [President Barack]
Obama is it's too late to do anything inside the Beltway. You
gotta take your case to the American people, mobilize them,
and organize them at the grassroots level in a way that we have
never done before." That became the basis of his populist call for
a "political revolution where millions of people get involved in
the political process and reclaim our democracy by having the
courage to take on the powerful corporate interests whose greed
is destroying the social and economic fabric of our country."

Whenever he was asked about socialism during his first
years in the Senate, Sanders would refer to what Scandinavian
countries had accomplished. When the topic came up again in
an October 2015 debate with presidential primary opponent
Hillary Clinton, Sanders pointed out what "countries like Denmark, like Sweden and Norway . . . have accomplished for their
working people." Clinton responded, "We are not Denmark."

Days later, historian Eric Foner penned an open letter to
Sanders in the *Nation* suggesting that he look toward American

58   history and not abroad in explaining democratic socialism. "Your response inadvertently reinforces the idea that socialism is a foreign import. Instead, talk about our radical forebears here in the United States." Foner described a history of radicalism that began with Tom Paine and continued through Frederick Douglass, Lincoln, the Populists, the Progressive Party, and Roosevelt's Second New Deal. "Your antecedents include not just FDR's New Deal but also his Second Bill of Rights of 1944, inspired by the era's labor movement, which called for the government to guarantee to all Americans the rights to employment, education, medical care, a decent home, and other entitlements that are out of reach for too many today." Foner explained that socialism "today refers not to a blueprint for a future society but to the need to rein in the excesses of capitalism, evident all around us, to empower ordinary people in a political system verging on plutocracy, and to develop policies that make opportunity real for the millions of Americans for whom it is not." Foner was situating the struggle for socialism within capitalism.

Foner did not talk to Sanders, but *Nation* editor Katrina Vanden Heuvel, who was a friend of Sanders's, sent him Foner's article. Another friend of Sanders's, historian Harvey Kaye, the author of a book on Roosevelt, was making the same case to the senator. Sanders responded. In a speech at Georgetown University the next month, he invoked Roosevelt and the Second Bill of Rights. Socialism, he explained, "builds on what Franklin Delano Roosevelt said when he fought for guaranteed economic rights for all Americans." In June 2019, at George Washington University, Sanders took the same tack. "In 1944, FDR proposed an economic bill of rights but died a year later and was never able to fulfil that vision. Our job, seventy-five years later, is to complete what Roosevelt started."

Critics of Sanders, including former Obama administration budget official and law professor Cass Sunstein, asserted that "Roosevelt was no socialist." But it is hard to deny that in Roosevelt's Second New Deal of 1935–36 (which established, among other things, a steeply progressive income tax, social security, and the National Labor Relations Board) and in his proposals for a Second Bill of Rights, Roosevelt was attempting, whether wittingly or not, to "rein in" capitalism. Roosevelt was enhancing the power and wealth of labor at the expense of capital. By citing Roosevelt's Second Bill of Rights, Sanders was making an argument for democratic socialism that began with Berger (with an assist from Bernstein), and went through Roosevelt and the Democrats of the New Deal. It was an important bid to give voice to millions of young people who, unbeknownst to most of their Cold War generation elders, had become deeply disillusioned with capitalism and, in looking for a political alternative, were receptive to a politics that called itself "democratic socialist."

Sanders combined an appeal to economic democracy with a moral appeal to community that evoked his earlier years in Vermont as well as the ideals of Christian and utopian socialists. Citing Martin Luther King, Sanders said, "I believe that the goal of human life, that you are richer emotionally as a human being, when we have a community, when we care about each other, when we love each other, when we are compassionate— not when we are stepping on other people." At a rally in Queens, Sanders asked his audience, "Are you willing to fight for that person who you don't even know as much as you're willing to fight for yourself?"

In the fall of 2015 and again in the fall of 2019, I asked participants at Sanders's rallies in New Hampshire, Virginia, and Nevada what they thought about socialism. Many were young people, but there were also a scattering of grandparents who had been around in the sixties. What I heard was dissatisfaction with capitalism and support for Scandinavian-style socialism. I also heard echoes of a Christian socialist commitment to cooperation rather than competition and to the community rather than to the individual:

"We care for each other. That's socialism."

"Bernie is a democratic socialist. That doesn't scare me. It inspires me. Because Bernie has recognized for a long time that our democratic political system is corrupt and leaving people behind. We need a government that is for the people. We aren't going to be rid of this label. It means making sure our economic and political system works for everybody."

"I'm a public-school teacher. I'm a socialist." (This was stated as if being a public school teacher *entailed* her being a socialist.)

"It means social services."

"I've thought of myself as a socialist for years. I think of community, of looking out for everybody, not just for yourself."

"I think socialism is scary for a lot of people. But I think capitalism is scarier. We need social programs, childcare, Medicare

for All, we need all these things to make society better. In
Sweden they don't say this will destroy the country. They
have higher taxes, but they don't have these concerns about
losing your homes."

Not a single person told me that socialism meant anything
like "public ownership and control of the means of production."
Sanders had shaped how his supporters thought of socialism,
but he was also responding to their own inclinations about
what was wrong with capitalism and what needed to be done
about it.

Perhaps the clearest sign that Sanders's concept had taken
hold was the rise of Congresswoman Alexandria Ocasio-Cortez.
In 2016, Ocasio-Cortez, who was working as a bartender and had
not been active in electoral politics before, was inspired to ring
doorbells for Sanders's campaign during the New York primary.
Two years later, recruited by some former Sanders staffers, she
ran for Congress, and to her own surprise, she defeated powerful
ten-term incumbent Joe Crowley, the fourth-highest-ranking
Democrat in the House. Members of DSA had walked the streets
for her, and halfway through her campaign, she joined DSA and
identified herself as a "democratic socialist."

When she went to Congress in 2019 and was asked what
it meant to be a democratic socialist, she echoed Sanders's
view. When "millennials talk about concepts like democratic
socialism," she explained to *Business Insider*, "we're talking
about countries and systems that already exist that have already
been proven to be successful in the modern world. We're talking
about single-payer health care that has already been successful
in many different models, from Finland to Canada to the UK."

62   Sanders's Last Campaign

Sanders was denied the presidential nomination in 2020 for the second and likely the last time—he will be eighty-three on Election Day 2024. Various political analysts attributed his loss to a host of tactical errors, but the real problem was a familiar one in American politics. The American two-party system makes electability a factor in choosing a presidential nominee. When the opposing nominee is someone who is seen to be formidable and very dangerous, as Democrats saw Trump in 2020, then electability becomes the principal concern. Whether voters actually supported Sanders or not, many saw him, because of his leftwing stands and reputation as an outsider, as less electable than former vice president Joe Biden.

Sanders's chances also suffered because many voters over forty-five were unwilling to support a candidate who identified himself as a "democratic socialist." Still others objected to programs like Medicare for All, which wouldn't benefit them if they already had private insurance or were on Medicare, and might significantly raise their taxes. In the end, Sanders could not overcome these reservations.

But even after the Democratic primary was essentially decided, Sanders continued to attract younger voters. He won a plurality of young voters even in states he lost decisively to Biden. And while Sanders's stand on Medicare for All probably hurt him during the primaries, the onset of COVID-19 and the massive loss of private health insurance by laid-off workers lent his plan an added plausibility. Arguments about spending too much for jobs and education that were used against Sanders also looked hollow in the wake of Congress's spending on the pandemic depression. To some extent, Sanders won the Democratic debate in 2020, but after he had already lost the nomination.

Sanders's political success was signaled by Biden's willingness to involve Sanders and his supporters in a set of task forces that were mandated to shape the Democratic platform and, if Biden were to win the presidency, his transition to office. Each task force was co-chaired by a Sanders ally and a Biden supporter. These included two of Sanders's surrogates during the campaign, Ocasio-Cortez and Rep. Pramila Jayapal, co-chairing the climate task force and the healthcare task force, respectively. Biden also displayed a recognition that, in the face of the pandemic depression, he would have to opt for the kind of "structural" change that Sanders and Warren had advocated in the campaign.

Socialism
After Sanders

If a new political tendency wants to gain influence in Germany or Spain, it will aspire to establish its own party. That was the path taken by the rightwing Alternativ fur Deutschland in Germany and the leftwing Podemos (now Unidos Podemos) in Spain. But in the United States, it is virtually impossible to start a new major party. That last happened in 1854.

Instead, new political tendencies have to gain influence by establishing dense networks of politicians, organizations, think tanks, publications, donors, dedicated supporters, and voters that can eventually dominate one of the major parties. That is how the conservative movement, which dates back to the 1950s, came to dominate the Republican Party in the last two decades of the twentieth century. With Sanders out of the presidential race, what are the prospects of a socialist tendency establishing this kind of network and gaining influence in American politics?

Heather Gautney, who was a senior aide to Sanders, wrote me after Sanders had dropped out of the race, "Sadly, I think that Bernie's exit means the 'socialist turn' will disappear from the

mainstream of American politics unless he creates a new political organization to carry the torch." Insofar as it is doubtful
that the seventy-nine-year-old Sanders will create a new organization, Gautney's prediction about the future of American
socialism might turn out to be true.

But the future for socialism actually looks far less bleak.
Growing support for socialism, particularly among the young,
predated Sanders's 2016 campaign. In May 2015, as Sanders's
presidential campaign was just beginning, and as most voters
didn't know who he was, YouGov found in a poll that 36 percent
of Americans between ages 18 and 29 had a "favorable view" of
socialism. In all, 26 percent of Americans had a favorable view.
And 43 percent of Democrats had a favorable view of socialism.
The conditions that led to this support for socialism and skepticism about capitalism have, if anything, been reinforced by the
pandemic and economic depression.

Where it may look bleak is in the socialists' lack of an effective political infrastructure that can mobilize and expand the
universe of Sanders's supporters. There are only a handful of
socialist politicians in Washington. There is one significant
socialist organization, the DSA. There are a score of socialist
publications and podcasts, but no think tanks and no policy
groups. DSA itself has helped elect promising local officials,
and its overall membership accords with Sanders's democratic
socialism, but orthodox Marxists have great influence over the
group's activist core and national leadership as well as over
America's main socialist publication, *Jacobin*.

What may redeem the promise of American socialism over
a decade or so is the existence of a dense network, comparable
to the conservative network of the 1970s, of "progressive" or

66   "liberal" national politicians, organizations (including labor unions), think tanks, and policy groups that endorse much of the Sanders program, but are still unwilling to identify themselves and their platform as "socialist." They and their successors, more than today's self-identified socialists, may hold the future of socialist politics in their hands. They could eventually prove Gautney wrong.

Socialism's Popular Base

Over the last decade, there has been growing sympathy for socialism among Democrats, and particularly among the young, aged roughly from 18 to 40, including millennials (born between 1981 and 1996) and Generation Z (born after 1996). This sympathy showed up in Sanders's support in 2016 and 2020, and even to some extent in Warren's, and in the popularity of Ocasio-Cortez. In an *NBC/Wall Street Journal* poll in January 2020, 60 percent of Sanders's voters had a positive view of socialism, and only 4 percent held a negative view. (The rest declined to state.) Only 12 percent had a positive view of capitalism.

Sanders's support was concentrated among the young. In the 2016 presidential primaries, Sanders got more votes from 18- to 29-year-olds than Hillary Clinton and Donald Trump combined. In the Pew poll in January 2020 of Democratic candidates, Sanders and Warren supporters together accounted for 40 and 17 percent, respectively, of Democrats 18 to 29 years old. In the 2020 primaries where exit polls were taken, Sanders regularly won the 18- to 29-year-old vote, and only lost the 30- to 44-year-old vote in two Southern states. In Michigan, after Warren had dropped out and he was paired against Biden alone, Sanders lost the primary but won 74 percent of the

18- to 29-year-old vote and 52 percent of those aged 30 to 44. He enjoyed similar margins in Texas, California, and Minnesota.

In a YouGov poll done for Data for Progress in December 2019, 21 percent of *all* voters preferred socialism to capitalism, 55 percent preferred capitalism, and 24 percent were not sure. That 21 percent conforms to the percentage of the electorate that a Sanders–Ocasio-Cortez party might now fetch in a multi-party system like Germany's. Among Democrats, 38 percent preferred socialism, 27 percent preferred capitalism, and 35 percent were not sure. Among 18- to 29-year-old Democrats, 47 percent preferred socialism, 18 percent capitalism, and 35 percent were not sure. Among 30- to 44-year-olds, 47 percent preferred socialism, 28 percent capitalism, and 25 percent were not sure.

YouGov also asked Democrats to choose a label from among "liberal," "progressive," "moderate," "socialist," and "none of these." The poll found that 18 percent identified themselves as "socialists." That's a step beyond saying one preferred socialism over capitalism. About a third of the Democrats from ages 18 to 44 identified as socialists, but the percentages fell precipitously for those 45 and older. Identification as a socialist actually increased as millennials entered their thirties, suggesting these voters won't follow the venerable maxim that, "If you're not a socialist before you're twenty-five, you have no heart; if you are a socialist after twenty-five, you have no head."

Almost a third of Democrats who had graduated from a four-year college but not pursued an advanced degree identified as socialists; only about a sixth of those who had not graduated or who had an advanced degree identified as socialists. In other words, those who identified as socialists were probably from the

68 lower stratum of the college-educated. And those who thought of themselves as socialists were very likely to live in a city or suburb rather than in a town or in the country. The socialists were generally under forty-five, had graduated from college, and lived in big metro centers. But there were still significant numbers of socialists who had not graduated from a four-year college. They probably lived in metro areas. In analyzing voter returns from 1988 to 2000, Ruy Teixeira and I found that in the big metro centers, voters with some college but not four-year degrees voted for Democrats in roughly the same proportion as college-educated voters.

Education and Socialism
What is the highest level of education you have completed? By percentage of Democrats who identify as a "socialist."

No HS	3	2-year	17
High school graduate	16	4-year	31
Some college	17	Post-grad	16

Age Percentage of Democrats Who Identify as Socialists

18–29	26	55–64	12
30–44	32	65+	12
45–54	17		

If you look at Sanders's donors, who contributed an average of $18 to the campaign, there is a tilt toward professionals, but also a significant group of lower-paid service workers. The largest groups of contributors were software engineers,

teachers, and nurses, but the biggest employers of donors were
Walmart, Amazon (most of whose workers are not software
engineers), Target, and the U.S. Postal Service. At Sanders's rallies, I found many of the supporters who were attending or had
graduated from four-year colleges had gone to modest schools
like Granite State in New Hampshire or George Mason in Virginia, and not to Dartmouth or the University of Virginia.

There is very little polling on what Americans think that
socialism is, but what there is suggests that Sanders's democratic socialism reflected the prevailing sentiment. In September 2018, a Gallup Poll asked respondents what was "their
understanding of 'socialism.'" Overall, 57 percent of Democrats
and Democratic-leaning independents had a positive view of
socialism, compared to 16 percent of Republicans. Among Democrats and those who leaned Democratic, a majority consid-
ered "socialism" to mean greater equality and enhanced social
services, including "medicine for all." The rest of the alternatives were a grab bag that included being sociable and offering
a "cooperative plan." Only 13 percent of Democrats saw "government ownership or control . . . of business" as socialism. In
other words, Democrats who had a positive view of socialism
were likely to see it along the lines of Sanders's democratic
socialism and not along the lines of orthodox Marxism or
Marxism-Leninism.

Disillusionment with Capitalism

What accounts for the rising support for socialism and opposition to capitalism, particularly among the young? Besides the
Sanders presidential campaigns, there are three large events or
developments and one underlying trend. The most important

event is the Great Recession that began in 2008. It reinforced anxieties about capitalism and about economic security that had been building since the beginning of the twenty-first century. While the reaction to the recession spawned the Tea Party among many older Americans outside big metro areas, it provoked a spate of movements critical of capitalism among the young, beginning with Occupy Wall Street in 2011 and culminating in the Sanders and Warren campaigns.

The second is the specter of climate change. Many of the young harbor the same fears of the effects of climate change that earlier generations felt toward the possibility of nuclear war. According to a 2018 Gallup Poll, 70 percent of those age 18 to 34 worry a great deal or fair amount about global warming. Over half think it will pose a "serious threat" in their lifetimes. They blame climate change on the excesses of the fossil fuel industry and more generally on a capitalism run amok, and seek the arrest of it in a Green New Deal that would require massive government intervention in the private sector.

The third is Trump's election in 2016 and presidency. It has highlighted the irresponsibility of the "billionaire class" spawned by contemporary capitalism. It has also provoked a vigorous reassertion of a moral commitment to racial and sexual equality. The Black Lives Matter movement predates Trump's presidency, but the movements and the protests over police brutality that it helped lead were energized by Trump's casual bigotry and threats of repression. The protests have inspired doubts about what participants call "the system," a term that has a broader reach than simply the way local police departments are organized, and a call for equality that can extend to capitalism itself.

In addition, there has been a longer-term shift in the place of the college-educated young in the economy that has fueled doubts about the benefits of capitalism. College graduates went from about 5 percent of the labor force after World War II to about 35 percent in 2018. These young Americans hoped to find higher wages and what the '60s generation called "meaningful" work as salaried workers in industry and as professionals and managers. And they initially did. From 1991, for instance, to 2001, the gap in income between a male high school graduate and a male college graduate increased from $30,792 to $45,444 (in 2017 dollars). And there was a growing celebration of individual initiative, epitomized by the rise of the Silicon Valley startup.

But the standard of living of college-educated workers stopped rising around the time that the dot-com bubble burst in 2001. According to economist Elise Gould of the Economic Policy Institute, the average wage of college-educated workers was 2.4 percent lower in 2018 than it was in 2000. The decline in the college wage premium coincided with a stratospheric rise in the costs of higher education. The costs of obtaining a degree have risen 213 percent at public colleges and 129 percent at private universities from 1988 to 2018. That has in turn fed the astronomical increase in student debt—$1.6 trillion by 2019. Average student debt for the young rose from $17,297 in 2000 to $29,597 in 2015. The Great Recession accentuated the economic insecurity that the young experience. In 2010, the unemployment rate for 18- to 29-year-olds was 14.2 percent.

Just as factory workers at auto plants lost their assurance of lifetime employment at the end of the twentieth century, so, too, in the early twenty-first century did college graduates.

Some millennials have found themselves "job-hopping." Some have taken jobs in the new gig economy without benefits, or they have worked for Starbucks as the so-called "barista with the BA." One survey of 40 Uber drivers in Washington, D.C. found that 29 had graduated from college, and 13 of them also had graduate degrees. If young people want to have children, buy a house, and settle down, the costs of housing have become prohibitive. According to a study by the real estate firm Unison, millennials in Los Angeles with the median income would have to wait until they were 73 years old before they could afford to buy a house. The lack of secure employment also fed fears about the costs of healthcare and insurance.

There were also growing doubts, especially among those without advanced degrees, about finding "meaningful work." According to a McKinsey Study in 2013, 48 percent of college graduates were in jobs like those at Starbucks or with Uber that did not require college degrees.

Software developers who wanted to write "cool" code ended up working for huge companies that dictated what they did. Teachers who wanted to help their students learn were increasingly forced to teach carefully prescribed curricula in order to prepare their students for standardized tests and were subject to the whims of highly politicized local and state boards. In other words, young college graduates increasingly found their expectations for secure, remunerative, and meaningful work dashed; and they increasingly blamed capitalism.

The onset of the pandemic and economic depression reinforced all these doubts and fears. Trump's ineptitude and self-dealing highlighted the importance of government acting in the social interest. Elizabeth Warren captured the new mood among many Americans in a quip: "Ronald Reagan famously said that the most terrifying words in the English language are 'I'm from the government and I'm here to help.' In this crisis, we've seen that the most terrifying words are actually 'We're in a crisis and the government doesn't have a plan to get us out.'"

The news site Axios summed up the effects of the new crisis on Generation Z's view of government. "They or their parents could lose employer-provided health insurance in the middle of a pandemic. That could fuel their already strong support for progressive, social safety net policies such as universal basic income and Medicare for All. They'll have experienced the impacts of the biggest government bailout in history—and [according to a January Pew poll] 70 percent already think government should do more to solve problems." In the first three months of the pandemic, more than a quarter of Americans under 25 lost their jobs. The conditions that have led to doubts about capitalism and support for democratic socialism over the last two decades can be expected to endure for the time being and even increase in intensity.

The Socialist Network
Can this growing disillusionment be mobilized in a socialist movement that would have an impact on American politics comparable to that which the conservative movement has had? That requires national political leadership and a broad network of organizations and publications. From 2015 to 2020, Sanders and Ocasio-Cortez were the lodestars of this new socialism. Their success not only fueled interest in socialism, but also gave it political direction. But at age seventy-nine, Sanders, having lost the nomination, is unlikely to provide leadership for a

74   movement. Ocasio-Cortez has not been an outspoken proponent of socialism, only of socialist initiatives. She joined the
DSA belatedly and is not known to be active in the organization.
In the absence of new national leaders emerging, the task of
championing socialist ideas and politics will pass for the time
being to publications and organizations.

There are a host of publications that explicitly champion
socialism. The most important of these is *Jacobin*, founded by
Bhaskar Sunkara, the son of immigrants from Trinidad, in his
dorm room at George Washington University in 2010. By 2014,
it had 4,000 subscribers, which is respectable for a socialist
journal. By 2020, it had 50,000 and was getting over two million unique visitors a month on its website. Nathan Robinson,
a graduate student at Harvard, was inspired by Sunkara to start
Current Affairs. Historian Michael Kazin and several young
socialist intellectuals revived *Dissent*. There are also socialist
podcasts, including the Chapo Trap House, Season of the Bitch,
and the Trillbilly Workers Party.

Though there are several socialist organizations in America,
most of them resemble small religious sects. The only significant one is the Democratic Socialists of America. DSA was a
product of a merger in 1982 between the Democratic Socialist
Organizing Committee (DSOC) and the New American Movement (NAM), to which I had belonged. DSOC grew out of a split
in the old Socialist Party in the early 1970s between supporters
and opponents of the Vietnam War. DSOC, led by Michael Harrington, drew together socialists who had been leery of the new
left, but who opposed the Vietnam War and supported antiwar
candidate George McGovern in the 1972 election. NAM was
an attempt to create a socialist organization that rejected the

new left's descent into Marxist-Leninism and echoed its earlier
commitment to participatory democracy. DSOC was primarily
based on the East Coast, NAM in the Midwest and West Coast.
DSOC sought to realign the Democratic Party; NAM devoted
itself primarily to local organizing. Together, the groups had
several thousand active members.

When the merger occurred in 1982, the country was mired in
a deep recession, and the Reagan White House and the Republicans were on the defensive. Conditions seemed ripe for a revival
of the left. But within a year, the economy had begun to recover,
and in 1984, Reagan was easily reelected. The new organization
began to hemorrhage members and chapters. In 1987, its political director decided he was no longer a socialist and went off to
graduate school. When Bhaskar Sunkara went to his first DSA
meeting in 2007, he found it composed of "relics" who remi-
nisced about the battles between socialists and communists.

Sanders's campaign was a turning point for the DSA. In 2015,
Sunkara and another young socialist, Dustin Guastella, launched
a petition drive to convince Sanders to run for president. They
became instrumental in getting DSA behind Sanders's candidacy
that year. By the summer of 2016, the DSA's membership had
grown to 8,500. Trump's election then brought about another
spurt. On the day of Trump's victory, 1,000 people joined the
DSA. Between then and July 1, 2017, DSA gained 13,000 new
members. In 2014, the Austin, Texas, DSA chapter had 14 members; by the end of 2016, it had 700; by 2019, it had 1,300.

DSA's composition also changed dramatically. In 2013,
the average age of a DSA member was 68. By 2017, when DSA
conducted a survey of its membership, the average age was 33.
Almost every respondent was college-educated. Six of 10 had

76 a masters, Ph.D., or professional degree. Only 3 percent had blue-collar jobs. But 13 percent were unemployed—a clear indication of the plight of the college-educated millennials. Jonah Furman, who worked as a labor liaison in the 2020 Sanders campaign, described DSA as an organization for "downwardly mobile millennials." DSA has chapters in 49 states and the District of Columbia. The biggest chapters are in Los Angeles, the East Bay Area, Chicago, New York, and the Washington, D.C. metro area. About 10 percent of the membership live in New York City.

The pandemic and depression have brought a spurt in membership. About 15,000 new members joined from March to June 2020. Chicago's chapter gained 600 new members.

Most of the DSA's chapter activity is locally driven. Chapters have backed rent control initiatives; they have been active in unions and tried to organize new ones; they have promoted the Green New Deal, and worked with immigrant organizations on a campaign to abolish the U.S. Immigration and Customs Enforcement. Their most notable activity, however, has been in running candidates. Over a hundred DSA members hold political office. These include six Chicago city council members. In November 2018, DSA members won city council races in Colorado (Aurora and Boulder), Connecticut (Middletown and Wallingford), Indiana (West Lafayette), Massachusetts (Medford and Cambridge), and Michigan (Lansing). In 2020, DSA showed their clout in New York City races, contributing to three wins by new candidates in state assembly races and helping DSA member Jamaal Bowman upset incumbent congressman Eliot Engel in the Democratic primary, virtually assuring the DSA will claim a third member of Congress in the

November general election. (At its peak, the old Socialist Party
boasted two House members, Berger and a distant relation of
mine, New Yorker Meyer London.)

With Sanders's presidential campaign over, however, the
DSA faces a new challenge. As long as Sanders was running for
president, he defined what it meant to be a socialist—not for
every reader of *Jacobin*, but for the 10 million or so Democrats
who voted for him and for most of the people who told opinion
polls that they prefer socialism to communism and identify as
a "socialist." By backing Sanders, the DSA implicitly embraced
a post-Marxist democratic socialism. That potentially gave it
contact with a base of millions of voters, many of whom agreed
with all or part of Sanders's program, but not necessarily with
the label of "socialist." DSA's challenge is precisely to bring this
electorate around.

Berniecrats and Trotskyists

If you look at the DSA's membership of approximately 70,000,
there are probably 1,500 to 2,000 dedicated activists who live
and breathe the organization. Beyond that, there are about
15,000 members who go to at least several meetings a year and
can be called on to work on campaigns. (These numbers account
for the 24 percent of the organization that voted in the 2019 referendum on whether to endorse Sanders.) The other members
pay annual dues the way that they would annually contribute to
the Sierra Club or Planned Parenthood.

Many of the paper members and some of the semi-activists
are what Sunkara has called "Berniecrats"—they were inspired
to join the DSA by his campaign and share his view of socialism
as Scandinavian social democracy and as the fulfillment of

78   Roosevelt's Second Bill of Rights and an opposition to racial and sexual discrimination. Some of the activists and political officials among DSA's leaders have broken with orthodox Marxism. David Duhalde joined DSA's youth group in 2003 when he was at Bowdoin. After graduation, he was an organizer for the Young Democratic Socialists. He became DSA's deputy director in 2015, at a time when the membership exploded. After the 2016 election, he become the political director of Sanders's Our Revolution, and is now the vice-chair of DSA's Fund, which gives grants to organizations and publications. "I view socialism emerging through social democracy," says Duhalde. "I see a lot of striving for a social democracy in a [Eduard] Bernstein fashion that will one day become a socialist society. . . . I'm more concerned with building social democracy day to day than with what socialism looks like when we get there."

Khalid Kamau helped organize a Black Lives Matter chapter in Atlanta in 2015. In 2016, he joined DSA and worked on the Sanders campaign, becoming a convention delegate. That experience, he says, inspired him to run for city council in 2017 in South Fulton, southwest of Atlanta; he won with 67 percent of the vote. With the council merely being a part-time job, Kamau moonlights as a Lyft driver.

Kamau described himself as a "Christian, vegan-eating socialist." "At my church," he explains, "we had a young lady. She wasn't going to be able to go back to school because she couldn't pay her bills. We raised a thousand dollars to play her bills. That's socialism." When a DSA caucus proposed that the organization only back candidates who were declared socialists, he disagreed. "When we are involved in a campaign," Kamau, who was the chairman of Metro Atlanta DSA, said, "it helps if they are socialist. But if they are half-decent, that's fine. Socialism is about people being more important than profits." Kamau added, "To me the journey is more important than the destination." When I told him that he was echoing Bernstein, he said he didn't know about "evolutionary socialism."

Vaughn Stewart, thirty-one, is a state legislator from Montgomery County, Maryland. Originally from Anniston, Alabama, he and his wife moved to Maryland after he finished law school. He worked briefly with a downtown D.C. law firm, but decided to go into a politics. A member of the Metro D.C. DSA chapter, he credits his election in 2018 to DSA members knocking on doors for him. "For me," he says, "democratic socialism means more democracy in the workplace, more representation on corporate boards, or more utilities that are nationalized, with the hope that we can have permanent prosperity for all. My generation feels we were wronged and the villain is capitalism, and the alternative is socialism."

But DSA also includes its share of orthodox Marxists. Some joined DSA out of two Trotskyist organizations that originated from the group that Joel Geier and Mike Parker, who had been part of the YPSL chapter at the University of Chicago when Sanders was there, formed with Marxist theorist Hal Draper. This group, the International Socialists, later split into two small, disciplined sects: Solidarity, which still exists, and the International Socialist Organization (ISO), which disbanded in March 2019. Members of both groups have played a significant role in political debates in the DSA. David Duhalde calls them the "neo-Draperites."

Dan La Botz is the elder statesman of these groups. He remains in Solidarity, along with about a hundred other DSA

80   members. La Botz believes that socialism is a separate stage of history that can only be achieved through a revolution. "You don't get any of these things except through a violent upheaval that transforms the constitution and the country. I don't see incremental changes." He rejects the idea of achieving change through the Democratic Party. "I think it is a capitalist party. I don't think anyone can take it over," he explained. He supported Sanders, but he does not think he is a socialist. "I don't think Bernie was a social democrat. I think he was a New Deal liberal."

Some young DSA members became convinced by reading and discussion that orthodox Marxist socialism made sense. Arielle Sallai is a recent college graduate who lives in Los Angeles and has worked in the entertainment industry and at nonprofits. She is the chair of housing programs for the large Los Angeles chapter. "To me," she explained, "being a socialist means understanding the class project. It is the belief that workers should seize the means of production. Workers should control the means of production. For example, it is the abolition of private property." I asked her whether, under socialism, people could own their homes. "We should live collectively," she insisted.

These orthodox Marxists make up a large part of DSA's most active core. Many of them function through organized caucuses that take positions and run slates for national leadership. Bread & Roses has attracted these orthodox Marxists. It describes itself as a "caucus of Marxist organizers" and stresses the "centrality of class struggle." At the 2019 convention, it advocated a strategy of "class-struggle elections" that would have limited DSA to endorsing socialist candidates. It declares that "the Democratic Party is not and never will be a party of and

for the working class" and seeks, when the time is right, to break
off and form "a mass working-class party." This is the same position that Geier and Parker, who later formed the International
Socialists, were taking in 1962. It's worth noting that none of
the groups that grew out of that original Trotskyist organization have had any luck organizing "a mass working-class party."

The conflict between the post-Marxists and the Marxists
emerged clearly at the 2019 convention and has had repercus-
sions on how DSA has responded to Biden's winning the nomination from Sanders. At the convention, the delegates narrowly
defeated the Bread & Roses proposal to limit endorsements to
socialists, but they backed a related proposal from a one-time
member of Solidarity that the organization should not endorse
any candidate in the 2020 election except Sanders. "DSA should
make it clear that we will not endorse corporate politicians,"
Andrew Sernatinger declared.

At the time, the vote appeared to be aimed at Elizabeth
Warren, whose platform was very similar to Sanders's, but it
put the organization on record not supporting any challenger
to Trump but Sanders. *American Prospect* editor Harold Meyerson, who came to DSA through DSOC, commented afterward, "It's a good thing that organizations don't have children
or grandchildren. If they did, you could envision little tykes
(well, little infant prodigies) fifty years from now asking their
grandparent—the Democratic Socialists of America—'What
did you do in the war against the neofascist Donald Trump?'
only to be met by an awkward pause."

By early April, when Sanders conceded and endorsed Biden,
the nation was in the throes of the pandemic and depression;
to many Americans, the threat posed by Trump's potential

82 reelection loomed larger than ever. Some DSA members favored reconsidering the convention decision, but the National Political Committee rejected the idea. "We are not endorsing Joe Biden," it tweeted, without any explanation. Meagan Day, a member of Bread & Roses and *Jacobin*'s campaign correspondent, applauded the decision. "There's no way we would have caved to pressure and endorsed Biden," she wrote. *Jacobin* editor Sunkara, one of DSA's leading intellectuals, announced he would be voting for Howie Hawkins, a member of Solidarity running as the Green Party candidate.

David Duhalde acknowledged that if the referendum were held, "the broader membership would probably be okay if we endorsed Biden." Nathan Newman, a professor at CUNY, wrote, "That this decision was made without a vote of the membership is why I'm not renewing my DSA membership. I would bet if a full vote of the membership was done, members would endorse Biden to defeat Trump." But a month later, DSA's National Political Committee doubled down on its decision, voting 13 to 4 not to "ask members in swing states to consider voting for Biden." The political committee added, "We believe Biden's anti-Chinese xenophobic messaging & the allegations of sexual assault against him exemplify how corporate Democrats allow the advance of far-right politics, white supremacy, misogyny, and capitalism."

The DSA leadership, driven by orthodox Marxists and latter-day Trotskyists, downplayed the gravity of the choice facing the American electorate in 2020, with Biden as the only alternative to the man Sanders calls "the most dangerous president in the modern history of this country." Instead, they sought to make a statement about the capitalist nature of both parties. By doing so, DSA was cutting itself off not only from its own Berniecrats like Newman and from the several million Americans who have come to question capitalism, but also from the broader political universe of progressives, left-liberals, and leftists who may not call themselves socialist, but support socialist initiatives.

Longtime DSA member Leo Casey, the director of the American Federation of Teachers' Albert Shanker Institute, commented, "The November election is seen as absolutely pivotal and decisive in the mass popular left—unions—and in organizations of color, civil rights, feminist, environmental, immigrant rights, LGBTQ folk. If the response of the DSA is, 'Sorry, there is no socialist running so we are going to ignore it, and throw our energies into the battle for state representative,' it will be irreparable to the DSA." But the group's leadership was in the clutches of Marxist antediluvians who were willing to risk isolation from the people whose support they needed to build a popular socialist movement.

The Culture War

The historic task of socialists and the broader left has been to unite the bottom and middle of society around an agenda that shifts power and wealth from capital to labor. To do that, socialists have to find common ground around economic grievances and democratic aspirations. In the United States, that has always been made difficult by regional economic disparities (which fuel cultural differences) and racial and ethnic divisions.

In the U.S. today, one of the deepest divisions has been between the politics of post-industrial metro centers like New York, Chicago, or the Bay Area and the small and mid-sized towns in the Midwest and South that have been decimated over

84   the last forty years by the loss of industrial jobs and stable communities. The former, along with most college towns, have
been home to Democrats and liberals; the latter to the downscale whites who voted for Trump in 2016. There are significant
numbers of metro Democrats and middle-American whites who
agree on issues like Medicare and minimum wage. As political
scientist Lee Drutman found in his survey of the 2016 election,
the most dramatic difference between the voters from these
two regions is over sociocultural issues—gender, family, race,
nation, religion, guns, and immigration—not economics.

Just as socialists isolate themselves from the broader electorate by taking orthodox Marxist stands on economics and
politics, they cut themselves off by taking extreme positions on
cultural issues that go beyond a commitment to democracy and
equality. That holds even for winning the support of those who
consider themselves "progressive" or "liberal." The larger liberal electorate is fully supportive of gay marriage and opposes
job discrimination against transgender people, but is wary of
transgender activists who advocate the abolition of gender.
They support affirmative action and oppose any form of discrimination against African Americans, but they are not ready
to endorse reparations. They decry racial injustice in policing
and in the courts, but they are not ready to abolish prisons and
defund the police. They favor comprehensive immigration
reform, but they oppose open borders.

On each of these social issues, DSA takes the most radical stand. DSA has gone on record in favor of "open borders."
At its Atlanta convention in 2019, it backed a proposal for the
"uninhibited transnational free movement of people"—a proposal that, if carried out, would undermine popular support for

generous welfare programs, including Medicare for All. At the convention, DSA adopted a resolution for a "police and prison abolition" working group. During the protests against police brutality toward African Americans that began in the spring of 2020, DSA echoed the demand for "defunding" rather than "reforming" the police—a demand that, without footnotes of explanation, a majority of Americans opposed—presumably because they saw it as threatening their own safety. But DSA's national leadership went even further, advocating "abolition as the path forward."

DSA could certainly grow in size and influence in years to come—the combination of the coronavirus and depression and the specter of climate change will create greater skepticism about capitalism. Its elected officials, who have to deal with actual voters, and who are realistic about what the organization can and should accomplish, could lead the way. But for DSA to accomplish its objectives, it will need to wean itself away from orthodox Marxism and from extreme positions on cultural issues that reflect its own narrow social base rather than the aspirations of most Americans.

The Shadow Socialists

The heavy lifting of creating a "historic bloc" for democratic socialism may be done by politicians, publications, think tanks, and organizations that are not overtly identified as socialist. They form a shadow socialist network that is at least as powerful as the conservative network of the 1970s. Minus the label, their view of capitalism is similar to that of Sanders and to the young Americans who identify themselves as "democratic socialists," and they are promoting many of the same policies

86   as Sanders and Ocasio-Cortez, including the Green New Deal and Medicare for All, but they don't want to suffer the stigma of being identified as "socialist."

Many intellectuals of this kind describe themselves as "social democrats"—a label that has no currency in American politics. They include Robert Kuttner, a founder of the *American Prospect*, *New York Times* columnist Jamelle Bouie, and political scientist Sheri Berman. Kuttner, Berman, economist Joseph Stiglitz, and political scientist Dani Rodrik share Karl Polanyi's view of capitalism. "There is almost a Polanyi secret handshake," Kuttner says.

Stiglitz, who wrote the foreword to a new edition of *The Great Transformation*, calls himself a "progressive capitalist," and warned Democrats in 2019 of the political perils of nominating someone identified as a "socialist," but his prescriptions are consistent with the idea of establishing socialism within capitalism. Indeed, Stiglitz admits that the "new breed of American democratic socialists—or call them what you will—is simply advocating a model that embraces government's important role in social protection and inclusion, environmental protection, and public investment in infrastructure, technology, and education. They recognize the public's regulatory role in preventing corporations from exploiting customers or workers in a multitude of ways."

Key think tanks include the Economic Policy Institute in Washington and the Roosevelt Institute in New York. The Roosevelt Institute's "New Rules for the Twenty-First Century" is a blueprint for subordinating markets to social needs and changing the balance of wealth and power. It proposes to

rethink the markets-first approach in favor of a pragmatic
assessment [and] to deploy the power of government to
directly provide goods and services and tackle the chal-
lenges our nation faces; restructure the economy by writing
new rules that strike at the heart of today's concentrations of
wealth and power; and reform our political institutions, so we
can make both the private sector and the government work
for all of us again.

Key publications, most of whom employ socialists as editors and staff writers, include the *Nation*, the *New Republic*,
the *American Prospect*, *N+1*, *In These Times*, *Mother Jones*, and
the *Intercept*. Similarly, there are scores of organizations that
include socialists. After Biden secured the Democratic nomination, eight of these organizations, Alliance for Youth Action,
Justice Democrats, IfNotNow Movement, March for Our Lives
Action Fund, NextGen America, Student Action, the Sunrise
Movement, and United We Dream Action called on Biden to
endorse Sanders's agenda, including Medicare for All, a wealth
tax, and a Green New Deal. Other prominent leftwing groups
include the Working Families Party and People's Action. Much
of the labor movement has always been congenial to socialist
economic reforms. Meyerson, who has covered labor, estimated
that "at least half the union staffers under thirty in D.C., no
matter the union, think of themselves as socialists."

Many elected Democrats are socialists in all but name. Since
1932, the Democratic party has never been, strictly speaking, a
"capitalist party" or a "corporate party," as the orthodox Marxists in DSA assert. It has always been mixed in its loyalties to

88   labor and capital, and has included politicians whose primary loyalty is to the former rather than the latter. These politicians, often backed by organized labor, have proposed measures that would introduce elements of socialism within capitalism. In the House of Representatives, the Progressive Caucus, which Sanders and Congressman Ron Dellums, a member of DSA, founded in 1991, has 95 members. Its two co-chairs both endorsed Sanders for president. Its key agenda items are Medicare for All, a Green New Deal, and a wealth tax.

In the Senate, about one-fourth to one-third of the Democrats regularly champion bills that would shift power to labor. Sanders has now gotten 16 sponsors for the Workplace Democracy Act and 14 for Medicare for All. Senator Edward Markey got 14 sponsors for his and Ocasio-Cortez's proposal for a Green New Deal. Regulars on Sanders's bills include Warren, Sherrod Brown from Ohio, Tammy Baldwin from Wisconsin, and Jeff Merkley from Oregon.

During the Democratic primary, *Jacobin* drew sharp contrasts between Warren and Sanders, but their platforms were virtually identical. Warren emphasized the need for a wealth tax far more Sanders did. She also stood on picket lines and proposed putting workers on corporate boards, as well as federal chartering of corporations, which would allow the government to regulate corporate behavior. Earlier, she was responsible for the creation of the Consumer Finance Protection Board. In Barack Obama's first term, she was the principal critic of the administration's coddling of the financial industry.

Her foes on Wall Street discounted her claim to be "capitalist to the bone." "She says she's a capitalist, but she's not a capitalist. She's really a democratic socialist in some ways. She wants to fundamentally change how an American company is governed," financier Steven Rattner declared. Many of her supporters also saw through her protestations. "I'm for Warren," John Turner, a young debate coach at Dartmouth, told me. "What is important is the issue of equality. She has gone from being conservative Republican to a democratic socialist." When I reminded him that Warren described herself as a "capitalist," he said, "She has to say that. We don't have a vocabulary for democratic socialism, so it is hard. But the wealth tax fits that."

Sherrod Brown, who briefly contemplated a run for the presidency, is from Mansfield, Ohio, a town that has suffered from corporations shutting down or moving out. He has worked closely with Sanders in the past. They opposed trade deals that they believed would hurt American workers. Brown has proposed legislation that would reward companies for investing in American jobs and that pay a living wage. His bill would charge corporations a "freeloader fee" when they pay their employees so little that they have to go on food stamps and Medicaid. Like Warren, he steers clear of being identified as a socialist. When one writer suggested that he sounded like Debs, he said, "Jeez, don't put that down."

In July 2020, Biden's task forces issued their reports. They called for a large-scale industrial policy that would aid, but also direct, American economic development; energy policies to achieve a carbon-free economy by 2050; the creation of a "public option" for national health insurance that could be the opening wedge for a single-payer system; proposals to strengthen labor unions; and a redistributive tax increase on corporations and

90   the wealthy to fund the new programs and investments. These proposals represented a distinct leftward shift from the conciliatory liberalism of the Clinton and Obama presidencies to initiatives that would change the balance of power between labor and capital.

British Socialism and Nationalism

There are striking resemblances between the recent development of socialist politics in Britain and the United States.
The revival is concentrated among young people in large metro
areas and college towns; the leading issues have included climate change, growing inequality, student debt, deteriorating
public services, support for immigration and minority rights,
gender identity, and job security. Both movements were led by
septuagenarian veterans of the new left—Jeremy Corbyn and
Bernie Sanders.

But the difference is that in the case of Great Britain, there
has been a public discussion of socialism (not confined to the
academy and small journals) for over a century, and a major
political party, Labour, that since 1918 has at least been nominally committed to socialism. Labour, with a powerful union
movement underpinning it, actually has also had a chance to
put its very non-Marxist socialist politics into practice.

There may be a lesson for American socialism in Corbyn
and Labour's abysmal failure in the December 2019 elections.

92   This was due in large part to Corbyn and the Labour party's response to Brexit. That may seem peculiar to Britain, but it reflected a rejection of a nationalist outlook that had been key to Labour's success after World War II. Labour's rout may also have been due to the kind of sociocultural factors that have shaped the outlook of American socialists and have made it difficult to conceive of socialism as a majority politics.

The Origins of British Socialism

The British Labour Party was always the least Marxist of European socialist parties. It didn't even commit itself to socialism until 1918, 18 years after it was founded. British socialism began with Robert Owen's communal enterprises. In the late nineteenth century, as socialists began to organize politically, the two most prominent groups were the Christian Socialists and the Fabians. And to this day, both groups play important roles in British politics.

The British Christian Socialists, like their American counterparts, were primarily drawn from low church (Quaker, Methodist) Protestant denominations. Influenced by the theory of evolution, they conceived of God working his will in the world to create the Kingdom of God on Earth. They stressed the brotherhood or fellowship of man as the overriding ethical concern; they rejected class conflict as a means toward socialism. One of their early leaders was Ramsay MacDonald, who later became the first Labour prime minister.

The Fabian Society originated in 1884 as a spin-off from the Christian Fellowship of New Life. The Fabians were primarily Christian Socialists who wanted to work for immediate economic reforms. The society was named in honor of Roman

general Quintus Fabius Maximus Verrucosus who sought a
slow step-by-step victory, rather than a single climactic victory
against the superior Carthaginian army. Many of the famous
British socialist intellectuals and politicians belonged at one
point to the Fabian Society, including (atheist) George Bernard
Shaw, Sidney and Beatrice Webb, H. G. Wells, Clement Attlee,
Anthony Crosland, Harold Wilson, Tony Benn, and Tony Blair.

Its guiding philosophy was reform, not revolution. Eduard
Bernstein, who lived in London from 1887 to 1901, had been
inspired by the Fabians. There were political differences among
the Fabians, but they became known for their support for ame-
liorative social reform, including national health insurance,
and for the nationalization of industry. They were statists; they
were not enamored of actual working-class ownership and control. Shaw quipped that "an army of light is no more to be gathered from the human product of nineteenth century civilization
than grapes are to be gathered from thistles."

British Marxism was initially an import from Germany.
It only played a significant role during the Great Depression
when, convinced that capitalism would collapse of its own
accord and preparing the way for socialism, Harold Laski and
other Labour Party Marxists argued against Keynes's proposals
for bringing the economy out of its slump. During Labour's
brief time in power from 1929 to 1931, the debate over policy,
Keynes wrote, was polarized between "the pessimism of the
revolutionaries who think that things are so bad that nothing
can save us but violent change, and the pessimism of the reac-
tionaries who consider the balance of our economic and social
life so precarious that we must risk no experiments."

94   **Socialist Nationalism**

British socialism really came into its own in July 1945, when the Labour Party, led by an Oxford-educated lawyer, Clement Attlee, took office with a majority on a promise to establish "the socialist commonwealth of Great Britain." With Britain, once the proud leader of world capitalism, heavily in debt and its empire dissolving, Attlee abandoned the dreams of imperial Britain and focused instead on reviving the British nation. His was a combination of socialism and nationalism.

The Labour government established a National Health Service that employed doctors and owned hospitals and provided free healthcare to British citizens. The government nationalized about 20 percent of the economy, including gas and electricity, mining, radio, civil airlines, railroads, and trucking. It did so by creating public corporations that were run independently by boards of directors appointed by the relevant government minister. Labour's postwar nationalizations made no provision for including worker or union representation. It was government through experts as the Fabians had advocated.

In 1952, Aneurin Bevan, who as health minister had overseen the creation of the National Health Service and who was seen as the leader of the party's left wing, defended the Labour government's approach to socialism:

A mixed economy is what most people of the West would prefer: The victory of Socialism need not be universal to be decisive. . . . It is neither prudent, nor does it accord with our conception of the future, that all forms of private property should live under perpetual threat.

According to Bevan, a full-blown socialism would consist of "public property" being the dominant, but not the only, type of property ownership. It would not entail direct worker control and ownership of the means of production. The working class would be represented through the state. The Attlee government also broke from Marxist orthodoxy by promoting economic nationalism. Historian David Edgerton recounts in *The Rise and Fall of the British Nation* that, in its 1945 manifesto, the party's election year platform, the term "socialism" appeared once, and "socialist" twice, but "nation" and "national" nearly 50 times.

For Labour, putting Britain first meant abandoning the economic liberalism and globalism of free trade and the gold standard. "Leaving behind economic liberalism meant creating not just an economic border but increasingly a culture of national self-supply," Edgerton wrote. The Attlee government used tariffs and subsidies to boost British industry and agriculture, and kept in place wartime capital controls to discourage the export of capital. And the strategy worked. Britain, which had relied on food imports since the repeal of the Corn Laws in 1846, became self-sufficient in agriculture. By 1950, a reviving British economy was leading the world in car exports and had the world's highest proportion of workers engaged in manufacturing. Stalin and the Nazis robbed the term "national socialism" of any except the most heinous connotations, but what the Attlee government did combined a commitment to democratic socialism with one to economic nationalism.

In 1951, Labour lost its parliamentary majority to the Conservatives, even though it won a higher percentage of the popular vote. Labour did not return to power until 1964 under economist Harold Wilson. Wilson had little interest

96   in expanding public ownership beyond renationalizing steel. Instead, Wilson stressed what he called "democratic" and "socialist" planning. He established a new Ministry of Technology and Department of Economic Affairs to promote economic growth. He increased funding for universities and established polytechnics. But in 1970, with the economy having slowed down, and the government forced to devalue the pound, Wilson lost a close election to the Tories.

Out of power, Labour moved left under the leadership of Tony Benn, who became chairman of Labour's National Executive Committee. Benn, the son of a former Labour MP and of a feminist theologian, was a Fabian and Christian Socialist who wrote that his socialism "owes much more to the teachings of Jesus . . . than to the writings of Marx, whose analysis seems to lack an understanding of the deeper needs of humanity."

As Wilson's Minister of Technology, Benn had embraced the prime minister's emphasis on economic growth rather than public ownership. But out of office, he moved leftward. Benn was impressed by a "work-in" at the Clyde Shipyards, where the workers, in defiance of a government plan to shut down the yards, kept on the job until the Tory government gave in and submitted a plan for maintaining the shipyards. Benn also fell under the sway of new leftists from the Trotskyist International Marxist Group who established an Institute for Workers' Control. In 1971, Benn outlined a plan for "industrial democracy" to entrust "individual firms to the people who work in them."

In 1973, the Labour Party, urged on by Benn, issued a program drafted by socialist Stuart Holland that combined a call for industrial democracy with extensive nationalization and planning. A National Investment Bank would purchase controlling shares in the 25 largest corporations; and the government would assert its power to oversee the investments of a hundred other corporations. Wilson, who had remained party leader, was unenthusiastic. When Labour regained Downing Street the next year, Wilson installed Benn as the Secretary of State for Industry, a position that would presumably put him in charge of implementing the manifesto. But industry pressure and opposition from civil servants led to Wilson ignoring the plan.

Benn had opposed Britain's entry in 1973 into the European Economic Community (EEC), the precursor of the European Union, under the Conservatives, and in 1975 Labour held a referendum on whether Britain should remain in it. Wilson allowed his ministers to vote their conscience, and Benn led the opposition to the EEC, charging that it was a "capitalist club" that would restrict Britain's ability to protect its industries. But with Labour divided and the Tories united in favor of remaining in the EEC, the referendum passed easily with 67.2 percent of the vote. Benn had been repudiated and was subsequently demoted from Secretary of State for Industry to Secretary of State for Energy. The affirmation of Britain's entry into the EEC and demotion of Benn spelled the end of British socialist nationalism.

Rolling Back Socialist Nationalism

Margaret Thatcher, who held office from 1979 to 1990, was a classical proponent of the free market. She believed in the employers' side of what Polanyi termed the double movement of capitalism. She set out to destroy what the Labour Party had wrought since 1945. That included nationalizations, union advances, and local control of taxes and public investments. To the extent that Labour had created countervailing institutions—the hallmark of socialism within capitalism—she wanted to destroy them. "We have done more to roll back the frontiers of socialism than any previous Conservative government," Thatcher boasted in 1982 at the Conservative Party conference.

In six successive acts from 1980 to 1990, Thatcher made it increasingly difficult for labor unions to organize and to strike. Due in good part to these acts, labor union membership fell from 11,498,000 in 1979 to 9,585,000 in 1991—from over 50 percent to less than 35 percent of workers. That reduced the power of unions to determine wage and working conditions within industries as well as weakening the Labour Party, which depended on organized labor for votes, money, and electioneering.

Thatcher sold off the industries that the Labour Party had nationalized, including British Aerospace, British Telecom, British Gas, British Steel, British Shipbuilders, and electric and gas utilities. She even sold off government research institutes, such as the Plant Breeding Institute. She slashed spending on education and housing, skewed the tax code toward the wealthy, and transferred the power of local governments, which were often in Labour Party hands, to the national government.

Thatcher repudiated the Labour Party's economic nationalist agenda, which to a great extent prior Conservative governments had shared. She removed capital controls on currency convertibility and on foreign investment and allowed foreign investors to buy British assets, including banks, at their pleasure. Her "big bang" deregulated London's banking industry. According to a BBC report 30 years later, the big bang produced "a free-for-all as brokers, jobbers, and the City's traditional merchant banks merged. Some were bought by UK clearing banks but many more were snapped up by much bigger U.S., European, and Japanese banks."

Disadvantaged by an overvalued pound caused by high interest rates and by government neglect, British manufacturing sharply declined. Britain became a net importer of manufactured goods and of foodstuffs. London, buoyed by the growth in financial services, became wealthier, while the towns and cities, particularly in the North, that had been devoted to manufacturing and mining went into arrears. Thatcher was forced out of office by her own party in 1990—ironically—over her refusal to join the European Exchange Rate Mechanism, the precursor of the Euro. There were limits to Thatcher's abandonment of the national economy. She was replaced by John Major, who, racked by a succession of scandals, was defeated for reelection in 1997 by Labour candidate Tony Blair.

Tony Blair and the Third Way

Tony Blair and his Chancellor of the Exchequer, Gordon Brown, temporarily resurrected the Labour Party's electoral fortunes— Blair and then Brown would hold office from 1997 to 2010—and they also shored up some parts of the British welfare state. Blair introduced a minimum wage that aided the poor and put money back into education. But with respect to British socialism and its national agenda, they represented a continuation of Thatcher's policies. When asked what her greatest achievement was, Thatcher responded, "Tony Blair and New Labour. We forced our opponents to change their minds."

Blair and Brown let Thatcher's financial deregulation stand. Brown went a step further. He took the Bank of England, which had charge of monetary policy, and the Financial Services

100   Authority, which oversaw the banks, out of Treasury and made them independent agencies, removing them from direct public accountability. Instead of funding infrastructure improvements with public money through taxes, Blair slashed corporate taxes and used Private Finance Initiatives (PFIs) to finance school, hospital, road, and other myriad repairs. Businesses provided the capital in the form of long-term loans with generous interest that taxpayers would have to pay back over 20 or 30 years. The FPIs, as the *New Left Review*'s Robin Blackburn wrote, "brought a deterioration in public-sector service standards and democratic accountability."

With a large majority, Blair could have repealed the employment laws that Thatcher had passed to hamstring labor unions, and realtered the balance of power between capital and labor, but he never attempted to do so. Convinced that Thatcher's defeat of the miners' strike in 1984–85 had cemented her popularity, he distanced the party and prime ministership from labor unions by ignoring the party institutions like the National Executive Committee where unions had influence and by soliciting business political funding to reduce the party's reliance on union money. He didn't re-nationalize the firms that Thatcher had sold off.

Blair had promised "a new Britain" and "a nation with pride in itself," but ended up binding Britain's economy closer to that of a German-led Europe and its foreign policy to an American-led imperium. Blair followed Major's, but not Thatcher's, lead by locking Britain into the EU, including its immigration and asylum policies. Blair actually hastened the influx of unskilled or semi-skilled Eastern Europeans into Britain, which helped precipitate the crisis over Brexit.

Blair and American president Bill Clinton advocated a "third way"—in Blair's case, between socialism and Thatcher's laissez-faire capitalism. They endorsed spurring growth through outsourcing and financial deregulation—an approach to finance that helped pave the way for the Great Recession. As prime minister, Blair joined Clinton in proselytizing for globalization—an approach that was antithetical to the socialist nationalism that the Labour Party had embraced after World War II. "I hear people say we have to stop and debate globalization," he said in a 2005 speech. "You might as well debate whether autumn should follow summer."

In 2007, Brown succeeded Blair, who had worn out his welcome by gulling the public about the threat of Iraqi "weapons of mass destruction" and committing British forces to the ill-fated American invasion of Iraq. If Brown had called an election that year, he might have won, but he waited until 2010, during the throes of the Great Recession. Blamed in part for Britain's financial crash, Brown lost to Tory David Cameron. Cameron, following the lead of Thatcher during the deep 1979 recession, cut spending and raised taxes. As a result, Britain didn't really escape negative growth until 2013. While Cameron's policies had made things worse, much of the public still blamed New Labour for the recession, and in 2015, with the economy finally picking up, Cameron easily defeated Labour candidate Ed Miliband. Miliband resigned as party leader after the defeat, and he was succeeded, to the astonishment of Labour's members of Parliament, by Jeremy Corbyn.

The Rise of Jeremy Corbyn

In 2013, Miliband had accepted the recommendation of a commission that the party should choose its leader by an overall vote of the membership rather than the current method of giving members a third of the vote and apportioning unions and Labour members of Parliament a third each of the vote. Blair and New Labour favored the change because they thought it would help distance the party from union control. In addition, Miliband recommended giving those who pledged support for the party's principles and paid a modest fee a chance to vote in the leadership election.

None of the initial candidates to succeed Miliband came from the MPs who had opposed New Labour. At a meeting, leftwing Labour MPs, having failed to recruit more prominent candidates, chose Corbyn, a crusty, little-known, rebellious backbencher, to represent them. In his campaign for the leadership, Corbyn denounced the Tory austerity and repudiated his own party's participation in the Iraq war. He appealed for a type of society where "we each care for all, everybody, caring for everybody else; I think it's called socialism."

Britain's mainstream papers, including the *Guardian* and *Financial Times*, adamantly opposed his candidacy. Blair warned that the Labour Party was in "mortal danger." But Corbyn was able to sidestep the major papers and the Labour Party's established leadership. He and John McDonnell, who managed his campaign, and his campaign staffers recruited 16,000 volunteers. They waged a campaign over social media. And two of the major unions hoping to "break the grip of the Blairites" backed him.

Inspired by Corbyn and his attack against Cameron's austerity, 183,658 joined the party from May to September,

and another 110,827 purchased voting rights as supporters.
Corbyn won 59.5 percent of the vote. One post-mortem
described Corbyn's recruits as "a coalition of idealistic youngsters, anti-austerity union activists, and grizzled left-wingers
returning to the party they quit in disgust under Blair." Vernon
Coaker, who ran one of the rival campaigns, attributed Corbyn's
success to his appealing to a "moral sense of purpose rooted in
Methodism, rooted in Christian socialism, rooted in the Lev-
elers. . . . Jeremy's got that at the same time as other Labour
people have lost it."

In the wake of Corbyn's victory, McDonnell and Jon
Lansman, who got his start as a 24-year-old working on
Benn's 1981 campaign for deputy leader, decided to establish
a new organization that would mobilize the young volunteers
from the campaign. In October 2015, Lansman, together with
James Schneider, a recent Oxford graduate, and two school
teachers, Emma Rees and Adam Klug, created Momentum.
Initially an independent organization, it would eventually
become a formal part of the Labour Party in order to fend off
Trotskyist groups that wanted to use it as a recruiting ground.
Over the next six months, it would attract about 4,000 members through online petitions and would begin to build a rudimentary grassroots organization. Then came Brexit and the
attempt to unseat Corbyn.

A Sixties-Style Anti-imperialist

Corbyn was known as a protégé of Tony Benn, but it was not so
much of Benn the economic nationalist, but of Benn who, after
he lost the race for the party's second-in-command in 1981,
increasingly turned his attention to foreign affairs. Corbyn,

born in 1949, first became involved in politics through the Campaign for Nuclear Disarmament, where much of the British new left of the sixties cut their teeth. When he graduated from high school, he joined the British equivalent of the Peace Corps, the Voluntary Service Overseas, and was sent to Jamaica to teach school. He later toured Latin America, where he became enamored of the Latin American left. (His second and third wives both came out of the Latin American left.)

He returned to England and settled in North London, where in 1983 he was first elected to Parliament. His main focus was foreign affairs, where he espoused a sixties-style anti-imperialism directed at the U.S. and his own country. He backed Fidel Castro in Cuba, Daniel Ortega in Nicaragua, Hugo Chavez in Venezuela, Nelson Mandela in South Africa (Corbyn was arrested several times in anti-Apartheid demonstrations), and the Palestinian opposition to the Israeli occupation. In 1984, he and Benn got in trouble with Labour leadership for inviting Sinn Fein leader Gerry Adams to Parliament during the Irish Republican Army's war against the British in Northern Ireland. He opposed Blair's and Clinton's bombing of Iraq in 1998, and was a founder of the Stop the War Coalition against the British and American invasion of Iraq. In 2015, before he was recruited to run for leader, he was hoping that the new party leader would appoint him to the Foreign Affairs Select Committee.

Over the years, he deferred on domestic questions to his friend and ally John McDonnell. McDonnell, the son of a Liverpool dockworker, went to a night school college and later got a master's degree in politics, and became a policy advisor in the early 1980s to the radical Greater London Council before Thatcher shut it down. In 1997, he was elected to Parliament.

When asked in 2006 what were his greatest influences, he cited, "Marx, Lenin, and Trotsky." He would often describe himself as a "Marxist," but as his influence on Corbyn's economics would reveal, his positions were more in line with Benn's socialism of the early 1970s than with the *Communist Manifesto* or Lenin's *State and Revolution*.

Corbyn Accepts Brexit

In the 2015 election, Cameron had promised Eurosceptic Tories and supporters of the United Kingdom Independence Party (UKIP) that he would hold a referendum the next year on the United Kingdom's membership in the EU. Cameron expected the referendum to fail easily, but to his surprise, it passed, 52 to 48 percent in June. The vote cut across party lines with Tory middle-class voters teaming up with Labour voters in towns devastated by deindustrialization to pass the referendum. Tory and Labour critics of the result blamed it on white racism and imperial nostalgia. But as Edgerton convincingly demonstrates in his account of post–World War II Britain, British nostalgia about the past wasn't for the days of Queen Victoria, but for the postwar period after the empire was dissolved when Britain enjoyed national self-sufficiency under governments that urged people to "buy British."

There was a small group of Labour members, founded in 2010 and dubbed Blue Labour, whose founder Maurice Glasman campaigned for Brexit, but the majority of Labour's MPs had been in favor of remaining. Corbyn, who had earlier joined Benn in calling for Britain to leave the "capitalist club," backed "remain," but on the eve of the vote, he told a television interviewer that he was "seven or seven and a half" out of ten in favor of remaining in the EU. The MPs blamed Corbyn's luke-warm support for the referendum passing and also for Labour setbacks in local elections earlier that year. That June, 75 per-cent of Labour MPs voted "no confidence" in Corbyn, pre-cipitating a recall election. Corbyn was again believed to be doomed, but with Momentum, whose membership had dou-bled almost overnight after the announcement of the recall, taking to the streets and online, Corbyn got 61 percent of the vote against the recall.

As the debate over Brexit proceeded, Corbyn faced a dif-ficult choice. While many of Labour's new voters, drawn from young college-educated cosmopolitans, had backed "remain," Labour's older blue-collar pro-"leave" rank-and-file provided the decisive margin in two-thirds of Labour constituencies. If Labour were to oppose Brexit even after the referendum had won, it would risk these constituencies and any hope of a majority. With some unintended assistance from Tory prime minister Theresa May, who had replaced a chastened Cameron after Brexit had passed, Corbyn finessed the conflict within his political base.

In January of 2017, Corbyn upset the Remainers by declaring his support for leaving the European Union and elimi-nating free movement among the EU nations. He favored a "soft Brexit" that would preserve Britain's role in the single trading market, but allow the British to use "state aid," which had been forbidden by EU regulations, to rebuild its industry. In April, Theresa May, wanting a clear mandate to negotiate, called an election for June. At the time, Corbyn trailed May by as many as 24 points in opinion polls. But Corbyn had two advantages over May. First, by being for Brexit, Corbyn won the support of

blue-collar Brexit voters in Labour's traditional strongholds.
And by favoring a "soft Brexit," Corbyn won the support of the
young Remainers in London or Oxbridge who saw his plan as
preferable to May's hardline proposals for Brexit.

Secondly, Corbyn won the battle of the manifestos. Labour's
manifesto was in the Fabian tradition of Attlee's 1945 and Wilson's 1974 manifestos. It promised to re-nationalize rail,
energy, water, and mail services, all of which had fared poorly
in the private sector. It proposed to restore higher tax rates on
the wealthy and business to fund free childcare and elder care
and to prevent planned cuts in welfare and social security and to
end fees on university enrollment. At the same time, the manifesto acknowledged the complaints about open borders voiced
by "leave" voters. It promised to "protect those already working
here" by ending "the exploitation of migrant labour undercut-
ting workers' pay and conditions."

The Tory manifesto, on the other hand, ignored years of
growing resentment toward Cameron's austerity policies. It
stipulated that before receiving home health care, the elderly
would have to exhaust the value of their savings, including the
value of their homes. It also set new limits on social security
payments for pensioners. These provisions provoked an outcry.
May tried to revise them, but the damage was already done,
and she and the Tories sank in the polls. May barely edged out
Corbyn by 42 to 40 percent. If the election had taken place several weeks later, Corbyn would have replaced her as prime minister. If that had happened, the election would have seen a new
kind of majority coalition for Labour. Corbyn had solidified
his control of Labour, but as it happened, the election was the
high-water mark for his leadership.

Labour's Millennial Supporters

The 2017 election showed how Labour's political base was changing. Labour dramatically increased its margin among the young, the college-educated, the urban, and the black and minority voters. Labour got 31 percent of the 18- to 24-year-old vote in 2010; 43 percent in 2015; and 62 percent in 2017. In other words, over seven years, Labour doubled its percentage among the youngest voters. Labour got 30 percent of the 25- to 34-year-old vote in 2010 (less than the Conservatives); 36 percent in 2015; and 56 percent in 2017. If the vote had been held among 18- to 34-year-olds, Corbyn would have won in a landslide. The resemblance to Sanders's base is striking.

Labour also dramatically increased its vote among the college-educated. It went from losing this vote by a point in 2015 to winning it by 17 points in 2017, 49 to 32 percent. It also increased its vote in greater London from nine points in 2015 to 32 points in 2017; and among blacks and other minorities, among whom it took 73 percent of the vote. The reasons that drove young people to Corbyn and Labour were probably very similar to those that drove young people in the United States to Bernie Sanders. Their expectations of a future way of life had not been met. Their lives had proven less secure and stable than they expected. They were not confident their situations would improve. Wrote the late Mark Fisher, a hero to many of the activists in Momentum, "It is not an exaggeration to say that being a teenager in late capitalist Britain is now close to being reclassified as a sickness."

After the election, Momentum grew to 40,000 members and about 200 local groups, primarily based in England. In September 2018, a slate endorsed by Momentum won all nine open

seats on Labour's National Executive Committee. At the annual
Labour Party conferences, Momentum started a parallel fes-
tival of ideas, called "The World Transformed." By 2019, when
I attended the September conference in Brighton, TWT, head-
quartered in a big park and two gigantic tents, and attended by
thousands of Labour delegates and visitors, looked like something between a county fair and a campground revival meeting.

During Corbyn's time as leader, his followers tried to forge
what he called a "twenty-first century socialism" for Britain.
Labour think tanks, some old and some new—including the New
Economics Foundation and the Center for Labour and Social
Studies (CLASS)—issued reports and analyses and recommen-
dations for Labour's manifesto. Organizations like Extinction
Rebellion and Reclaim the Power sprung up to promote climate
change and a Green New Deal. *New Left Review* remained the flag-
ship of British socialism, but it was joined by webzines like *Red
Pepper*, *Open Democracy*, *Canary*, and *Evolve Politics*.

If there was an idea that united the different groups, it
was combating climate change through a Green New Deal—an
idea that had originated with Ocasio-Cortez and Senator Ed
Markey's plan in the United States. The Green New Deal was
seen as a way of addressing a major challenge to the planet with
an "ecosocialist" program that would require public ownership
and lead to full employment. Grace Blakeley, a fellow from
the pro-Labour Institute for Public Policy Research, framed the
choice as being between "extinction and utopia." Some of the
groups like Extinction Rebellion demanded a carbon-free
Britain by 2025; others settled on 2030.

There were also interesting attempts to resume the attempt in the early 1970s to go beyond the Fabian program for

nationalization. A group called "We Own It" devised complicated schemes for democratic ownership and control ("This isn't about nationalizing") of public transport, water, energy, and the Royal Mail. The Green New Deal embraced democratic planning of resource use. But as I found at the DSA convention in the United States, the proposals coming out of Britain's new left also reflected the age and social and economic circumstances of the people making them and were not really designed with the idea of creating popular majorities that would unite different parts of the population. They were based on faith rather than political calculation.

A prime example is the much-touted London-based Extinction Rebellion, which first made the news when it blocked bridges over the Thames in November 2018 to protest government inaction. Its demand for a carbon-free Britain in 2025 would have entailed replacing millions of automobiles and 90 percent of home heating devices, suspending air travel, and radically altering people's diet and work lives. Most scientists would regard 2030 as a radical and probably unattainable target without massive disruption and 2050 as a reasonable one.

There was no support at The World Transformed for Brexit. The young British left was squarely in the "remain" camp befitting above all their post-industrial metropolitan location at the center of globalized finance. Their analysis betrayed a contempt for British nationalism. It attributed support for Brexit to imperial nostalgia or anti-immigrant racism. There was no support for restrictions on immigration to protect workers from low-wage competition. On the last day of the Brighton conference, when the MPs had to leave for the opening of Parliament, the activists who remained passed a resolution on immigration

to "maintain and extend free movement rights"—a direct repu-
diation of Labour's 2017 manifesto, which had said "freedom of
movement will end."

The Socialist Manifesto

In June 2019, Theresa May resigned, having failed to win Parliament's agreement to a Brexit deal she had negotiated with
the EU. The Conservative MPs elected Boris Johnson, a former
journalist, mayor of London, and May's former foreign minister,
to replace her. After several false starts, Johnson finally got a
majority in Parliament to agree to the outline of a new Brexit
agreement he had negotiated with the EU, and to call for a new
election in December. Almost 20 points ahead in the polls,
Johnson wanted to use the election to give himself an unassail-
able majority to finalize a deal with the EU.

Over the six weeks of the campaign, Johnson and the Tories
remained well ahead except during the week that Labour issued
its manifesto. During that week, Johnson's campaign staff told
the *Financial Times*, Corbyn and Labour pulled within four percentage points of the Tories. That suggested that whatever
the electorate's opinion of Corbyn and of Labour's position on
Brexit, it supported the most radical manifesto that Labour had
ever issued. The manifesto backed widespread nationalization of the energy and transportation sectors and worker stock
ownership in their businesses. It proposed a new Ministry for
Employment Rights charged with "shifting the balance of power
back towards workers."

But when the novelty of Labour's manifesto wore off, the
Tories were able to reestablish their earlier lead. Conservatives routed Labour, winning 43.6 percent of the vote and 365

112   seats, to 32.2 percent and 202 seats for Labour. It was Labour's
worst showing since 1935. Labour once again won the young—
those 18 to 24 by 38 points over the Tories, and those 25 to 34
by 32 points. It also won those with a college degree or more.
But it lost the working class decisively. Labour won London and
the constituencies with a high percentage of professionals, but
was blown away in small and mid-sized towns, even ones that
had been Labour strongholds for almost a century. Labour lost
most of what had once been its working-class base and relied
for its support primarily on the younger urban voters who had
come into the party in the last decade. It ceased to be a "workers'
party" and became a party of college-educated cosmopolitans.

Reasons for Defeat

Labour might have lost in any case, but it lost decisively because
it abandoned the commitment to nationalism that had been at
the heart of the Labour Party's socialism since 1945. That was
evident in its failure to develop a coherent position on Brexit.
Under pressure from his cosmopolitan base, which favored
holding a second referendum on Brexit, Corbyn capitulated.
During the election, he promised to renegotiate in three months
a Brexit agreement and then hold a binding referendum on it—
in effect, to accomplish in three months what it had taken the
Tories three years to do. Corbyn wouldn't take a position on how
he would vote on the referendum, but his second-in-command,
McDonnell, made it clear that, whatever the results of Corbyn's
negotiation, he would vote for "remain." It was an utterly inco-
herent position, and also lacked any credibility.

     In the election, Labour lost "remain" votes to the Liberal
Democrats who promised to tear up Brexit and remain in the

EU and they lost Labour supporters of "leave" to the Tories and their slogan of "Get Brexit Done." Corbyn's approach, it became clear, was not capable of winning a plurality, let alone a majority of British voters.

Labour also lost because of Corbyn's personal unpopularity, but that factor was not unrelated to the stand Corbyn took on Brexit. The Tories were able to highlight Corbyn's various global allegiances to countries like Russia and Venezuela that had little good to say about Britain. Corbyn's old-style anti-imperialism undermined any attempt to appeal to British nationalism. Corbyn was also plagued by accusations of anti-Semitism in the Labour party, some of which were justified. Laura Pidcock, an MP who lost her seat, summed up the problem with Corbyn's candidacy.

> When I knocked on your doors in 2017, so many of you talked about what a good guy he seemed, that he was on the side of the people. . . . In 2019, you seemed so much angrier about Jeremy Corbyn. I had a handful of angry people say "I would shoot him" or "take a gun to his head" whilst in the next breath calling him an extremist.

Finally, Labour may have suffered from being identified with extreme positions on climate change, immigration, and gender identity. Two sociologists, Steve Hall and Simon Winlow, primarily known for their work on criminal justice, put the problem in this way:

> Convincing an electoral majority in the grip of post-crash austerity that a progressive economic project based on public

control of finance and investment is feasible would have been possible in an ambience of shared interests—prosperity, security, sustainability, and so on. Instead, the self-styled progressive liberal left relentlessly attacked the full spectrum of traditional institutions, beliefs, values, and identities.

After the election, there were troubling signs that the party's new left had still not absorbed the lessons of Labour's defeat. In January, as different candidates were vying to succeed Corbyn as party leader, a heated controversy between a small, newly formed transgender group and several venerable feminist groups made headlines. Momentum and its candidate to succeed Corbyn threw their support behind the transgender group, which was demanding that the party *expel* the two feminist groups that wanted to be able to limit their rape and shelter services to biological women. It was a powerful sign of how much the Labour Party had become hostage to a rarified cosmopolitan culture.

The question for Labour is whether it can develop a socialist politics that retains the support and enthusiasm of millennials in big metro centers and at the same time appeal to British voters who don't live in London or a university town and don't have advanced degrees and still carry with them a fondness for the British nation and for a non-Marxist socialism. The response to Labour in the 2017 election and to its manifestos in 2017 and 2019 suggests that the potential exists for a majority based on "shared interests" in "prosperity security, sustainability, and so on." But for Labour to succeed, it has to frame these proposals in a way that respects and doesn't denigrate British nationalism—a point that Jonathan Rutherford of Blue Labour made in his election post-mortem. "The democratic nation and its rule of law is the best means of safeguarding our rights and freedoms," Rutherford wrote. "And the nation state is still the best political unit to manage globalization in the interests of a democratic polity."

At the end of January, Labour chose the bland former Shadow Brexit Secretary Sir Keir Starmer as its leader. Starmer had been an outspoken proponent of "remain" and of a second referendum—exactly the stance that had contributed to Labour's downfall. But fashioning himself as a member of the party's "soft left," he pledged to unite the feuding factions. Under Starmer, Labour published in June a 154-page "Election Review" analyzing the defeat and proposing a way forward. The review acknowledged that "Labour lost support amongst all classes, but amongst the working-class communities the most."

Labour's prescriptions for the future consisted, however, of new processes rather than programs. It called for a "collective process of reflection and reconciliation" and a "series of training and listening events." It asserted that "Labour must be a well-led professional, innovative organization with a more inclusive culture" and "be connected with the communities and voters we want to serve." It insisted that "Labour must lead the debate about the different society and economy that must emerge from the coronavirus crisis," but it gave little hint of what Labour might advocate.

Labour's prospects appear dim. Johnson, unlike America's Trump, is an experienced politician who has chosen not to ally his party to rightwing populists. Instead, Johnson has drawn selectively on Labour's tradition of economic nationalism. His budget included generous state aid to rebuild the industrial areas of England and money to repair the National Health Service to fight the coronavirus. Johnson has also promised to restore Britain's self-sufficiency in agriculture and to promote a campaign of "buy British." "The impression left," the *Guardian* wrote, "is that we are all Keynesians now." To be sure, Johnson's budget excluded Labour's plans for redistributing wealth and empowering labor. Johnson remains a politician of the center-right, but one that is like the Tories before Thatcher. If he can dispel the public's doubts about his inept handling of the pandemic, he could give the Tories staying power against a Labour Party in disarray.

Brexit also looks better in the wake of the pandemic and depression. The EU was divided over aid to a tottering Italian economy and over Hungarian prime minister Viktor Orban's attempt to undermine his country's democracy. The pandemic has led countries to close their borders and to initiate "state aid" of their companies. Even a hardened advocate of a United States of Europe, Yanis Varoufakis, has admitted that Britain may have made "a rational choice for the wrong reasons." That serves as another reminder of how much Labour under Corbyn—in spite of its stand against austerity—lost its way politically.

Populism, Nationalism, and Socialism

This is the third book in a trilogy that began with *The Populist Explosion* and continued with *The Nationalist Revival*. There is a connection among these subjects. The revival of populism, political nationalism, and socialism is a product of a breakdown in the consensus on the virtues of the free market and of globalization that had prevailed from the 1980s until the Great Recession. The pandemic and global depression are the second, and perhaps the fatal, blow to this older consensus. Here is how the rise of populism and nationalism bears on the rise of democratic socialism.

Populism

Populism is a political logic, not a specific ideology like conservatism or liberalism or socialism. It's like the underlying chassis of an automobile that can be used to build a variety of car models. Populist appeals frame politics as a conflict pitting the people against the elites or establishment. These appeals can come from the left, center, or right. In 2016, both Sanders and Trump ran populist campaigns; in 2020, Sanders ran against the "billionaire class" and Warren against the "rich and powerful." In Europe, France's National Rally of Marine Le Pen and Germany's Alternativ fur Deutschland have appealed from the right; France's Insubordinate France of Jean-Luc Melenchon and Spain's Podemos from the left.

Populist appeals strike a chord with voters when a politics and policies that have broadly united the electorate don't live up to their promises and when the dominant political and business leaders in Washington or London or Paris refuse to acknowledge that circumstances have changed. The populist parties and candidates are an early warning sign that a new direction or a new consensus is needed.

A populist campaign is particularly appropriate for a democratic socialist in the current post-Marxist era. The adversary is the same—the ruling class, the establishment—but what had been for socialists the widely accepted agent of change—the industrial working class—has been eclipsed by a diversified and stratified and sometimes very divided collection of wage and salary workers. They can best be described in the language of populism as "the people," "the 99 percent," or "working people." When some of the newly minted or old-time Marxists use terms like "class war" or appeal to a mythical "working class," they are evoking a theory of revolutionary change that 150 years have disproven. (My former colleague James Weinstein, who belonged to the Communist Party for a decade after World War II, used to tell the story of the Communist candidate for office in New York City who began his campaign speeches by addressing, "Workers and peasants of the Lower East Side.")

The virtue of Marx's theory of class was that it combined sociology and politics. The working class, which was just then emerging, was at once a mutually recognizable social group and an historical engine of change. It was a class *in itself* and *for itself*. But while academic sociologists and orthodox Marxists can make elaborate sociological distinctions among and within classes in the United States or Europe today, they carry little political weight. So, too, does the pollsters' use of the term "working class" to refer to voters with "some college" but not a four-year degree. (Junior college graduates, unite!)

Some socialists have picked up the term "professional-managerial class" (PMC). In a debate in the New American Movement in the early 1970s, Barbara and John Ehrenreich invented the term to counter the view that post-industrial capitalism had spawned a "new working class" that included upper-level-white-collar workers. *Jacobin* used this term to distinguish supporters of Sanders (the true working class) from Warren's backers (the PMC). But the term is doubly misleading as a guide to socialist politics. It obscures the leading role of nurses and schoolteachers—both of whom the census classifies as professionals—in the labor movement and in support for socialism in the United States today. The nurses' union was one of the main supporters of Sanders's campaign. And it lumps them or software developers or the other workers with advanced degrees who make up a significant percentage of DSA's membership and Sanders's and Warren's donors in with corporate CEOs and Wall Streeters who are generally opposed to socialist reforms such as Warren and Sanders proposed in their campaigns. Populism has reemerged on the left precisely because of the fatuity of attempts to base a politics on a neo-Marxist class analysis.

120   Nationalism

In the United States and Great Britain, few on the left, let alone on the socialist left, understand why nationalism is an integral part of any socialist or economically progressive appeal. For orthodox Marxists, their view of nationalism bears the stamp of Marx, Lenin, Trotsky, and even Rosa Luxemburg. In his book *The Socialist Manifesto*, Sunkara quotes Luxemburg, "[The] Rights of Nations is nothing more than a metaphysical cliché." Attacks against nationalism are rife in socialist and leftwing journals. "There Is No Left Case for Nationalism," *Nation* senior editor Atossa Araxia Abrahamian declares. Blue Labour's support for national identity has been branded "bigoted" by its Labour foes.

In the United States, socialists and the left identify nationalism with Trump's America First. In Britain, Labour Party intellectuals identify nationalism with UKIP and the European right. "There is a simple reason why pandering to nationalism will, in the end, always benefit the right: it is a tool employed by the ruling class to maintain their power and put blame for their failings somewhere else," Sabrina Huck writes in the party's unofficial website, LabourList. In the United States, the disdain for nationalism extends to the sentiment of patriotism. "'Patriotism' is a Dead End for the Left," an article in *Jacobin* declares. In one Twitter poll conducted by a socialist writer, David Klion, only 12.3 percent of the respondents described themselves as "patriotic."

Strange as it may seem, a viable socialism must be nationalist. Its fundamental framework must be the nation and its citizens. For a democracy to function, its citizens must be clearly defined, their common commitment to the nation assumed.

But socialists can be oblivious to this very simple idea. At the
Labour Conference in Brighton, the "remain" faction proposed
that temporary residents from other EU countries be allowed
to vote in its national elections. That would be subversive to
democracy.

Similarly, proposals for an advanced welfare state and a
redistribution of wealth must rest on national boundaries.
They must recognize that in order for a citizen to accept, for
instance, "Medicare for All," they must be willing to pay high
taxes to achieve coverage not only for themselves but for people
they don't know and may never meet. If that latter group is not
clearly defined and not limited to a nation's citizens—if, for
instance, anyone who crosses the nation's borders can claim
coverage, as some of the Democratic presidential candidates
appeared to advocate during the 2020 primary—then many
people won't support such proposals. Why should they pay
their taxes to support people who don't share a common social
and economic obligation to the nation?

Finally, where employment is not boundless, nations must
protect the jobs of their workers by limiting immigration. If
unions want to organize low-paid service workers, they cannot
contend with a continuing surplus of immigrant workers eager
to compete with those already employed. During the 2016 presidential campaign, when Sanders was rebuked by Vox editor
Ezra Klein for opposing open borders, he replied, "No, that's
a Koch Brothers proposal," referring to the rightwing business agenda of using unrestricted immigration and a labor surplus to drive down native workers' wages. Much of the plight of
unskilled African American workers over the last 50 years was
due to competition from unskilled immigrants. But America's

122   socialist left is impervious to *any* restriction on immigration. "You can't talk about it," Dustin Guastella says.

When Sanders asked his supporters, "Are you willing to fight for that person who you don't even know as much as you're willing to fight for yourself?" the expected answer was "yes." But altruism has its limits. Our moral commitments go in concentric circles from family to friends to nation. They can extend to people of other nations, but not with the same intensity or commitment. Americans don't feel the same commitment to aiding the poor in Lahore (unless they happen to be Pakistani Americans) as they do to aiding the poor in Chicago. And the fact that they are willing to aid the poor in Chicago even if they live in Richmond, Virginia, shouldn't be trifled with by undermining our sense of common nationality. It's not just important for getting programs adopted; it's important for bridging the gap between America's disparate cultures.

None of this is to say that socialists and the left can't support international cooperation to address problems that a single nation cannot hope to address, such as climate change or the current pandemic, or that they can't support immigration or immigration reform. Or that socialists cannot be outraged by the Chinese regime's unconscionable treatment of the Uighurs. But when it comes to advocating a shift of power to labor and the expansion of democracy and equal rights, that must be done within the context of the nation. Much of the British Labour Party's failure lay in its abandonment of the party's commitment to economic nationalism and its equivocation on the subject of open borders. And American socialists will not be able to escape their own cultural insularity until they come to terms with what their own national identity means to their politics.

Socialism

In his masterpiece, *The Economics of Feasible Socialism*, the late Alec Nove, a Russian expatriate who became a prescient expert on the Soviet economy, contended that the idea of socialism "should be conceivable within the lifespan of one generation—say in the next fifty years; conceivable, that is, without making extreme, utopian, and farfetched assumptions." Marx's own ideas seemed feasible in the 1880s—the industrial working class was expanding rapidly, along with the labor movement, and Europe had been riven by revolutions since 1789—but have proved to be utopian.

Socialists today who talk vaguely of an economy based on public ownership and control of the means of production—the standard Marxist formulation—are engaging in utopian thinking. When I pressed a young DSA member on the subject of how that would apply, say, to the computer industry, he replied, "I don't have an opinion." In *The Socialist Manifesto*, Sunkara used the model of a pizza sauce company that is transformed from owner-controlled to worker-controlled to illustrate the promise of socialism. That's the kind of argument by example that Robert Owen was making for what in retrospect were his relatively small textile plants. It's not a model that is clearly transferrable to America's or Europe's large corporations.

To be politically relevant, the left's idea of socialism must be grounded in contemporary history. It need not, and can't be, an *inevitable* outgrowth, but it has to be a *possible*—and in the eyes of many—a *desirable* outcome. Citizens will not seek to replace capitalist with socialist institutions purely out of moral conviction. They have to believe that purely market-based institutions have dramatically failed to provide prosperity and

124   well-being to their workers and consumers. And they might not seek the full socialization of an industry. In many American industries, what is needed as a first step is unionization and regulation in the national interest—the assertion of what John Kenneth Galbraith called "countervailing power."

In the wake of the pandemic and depression, the healthcare industry certainly is a candidate for a partial public takeover. It has clearly failed. So, too, are parts of the transportation sector. And as the effects of climate change bear down, Americans, too, may finally decide to increase public control over energy production and use. Today's crisis has also laid bare the failure of the labor market to provide equitable and needed outcomes. Many workers who are now recognized to be "essential" to society, such as those in hospitals and meat processing plants, barely can support families, while hedge fund and real estate speculators, who do not make any contribution to society's betterment, live in luxury.

By dramatizing the inequality of wealth and power, the pandemic and depression have lent credibility to reforms that might have seemed too radical for the public to contemplate. These include some form of guaranteed annual income to cushion those at the bottom from recession and depression and to sustain consumer demand; a massive investment in public welfare, including schooling and healthcare (including universal, accessible health insurance); a publicly subsidized and directed industrial policy aimed at reviving American manufacturing, protecting the supply chains of vital industries, converting to renewable energy, and channeling the activity of the financial sector toward productive investment; universal access to broadband; and a radically redistributive

tax reform that undoes decades of regressive tax cuts on personal and business income.

Many of these reforms would shift power from capital to labor and make the country more democratic, and they are feasible within a generation given the power of a movement behind them. They are currently embraced not only by self-identified democratic socialists, but also by "progressives" like Warren and Brown, and by the Biden campaign, and in Europe by parts of the Green Parties and Social Democratic Parties. But to achieve them, socialists and progressives will have to abandon their dogmatic adherence to orthodox Marxism, their cultural insularity, and their contempt for national sentiment. They will have to focus single-mindedly on the profound weaknesses in the economy and the safety net that the pandemic depression has revealed.

The Polanyi Moment

We are experiencing a breakdown of capitalism similar to that which Karl Polanyi described took place between the two world wars. In the 1930s, protection against the vagaries of the free market and the collapse of the gold standard came through state intervention and the abandonment of the gold standard in favor of an economic nationalism. At the extremes, it took two very different forms—fascism in Central and Southern Europe and the New Deal in the United States. In Europe, several forays to the left in France and Spain were crushed by the right. In the U.S., Roosevelt was able to hold the right in check.

Today, the reign of globalization and market fundamentalism is also breaking down and leaving the average citizen unprotected, and perhaps with the onset of pandemic, even

126 more so than during the 1930s. The twin menace of pandemic and depression is calling forth the need for massive state intervention and a dramatic shift away from private to public power. But as in the 1930s, this can take very different forms. In China, India, Russia, Turkey, Hungary, and Brazil, it has reinforced trends toward rightwing authoritarianism. In the case of China, this could threaten peace in the Pacific region, as Xi Jinping and the Communist Party, unable to sustain rapid economic growth, gins up national rivalries with its neighbors and with the United States.

In Europe, the European Union, based on a promise of its upward economic convergence between North and South, and democratic convergence between east and West, is under stress, as countries in the prosperous North resist aiding those in the debt-stricken South, and as countries in the East, particularly Hungary and Poland, defy the democratic norms of the West. For the time being, France and Germany have been able to keep the peace, but in another variation of Jameson's quip, it is easier to see the end of the European Union than the end of European capitalism. How the countries of the European continent turn politically will depend on the fate of the EU.

In Britain and the United States, there is now widespread recognition, even by establishment forces, that capitalism must be tamed. In August 2019, the Business Roundtable, representing over 200 of America's largest corporations, issued a statement calling on corporations to help deal with inequality and to heed the needs of stakeholders and not just shareholders. In September 2019, the *Financial Times* began a series of articles calling for a "reset of capitalism."

That perception has also spread to Republican politicians looking toward 2024. Florida senator Marco Rubio and Missouri senator Josh Hawley have championed a new "industrial policy" that, in defiance of "market fundamentalism," would rebuild manufacturing in the ravaged towns and small cities of the Midwest and South. In Britain, Johnson and his Chancellor of the Exchequer, Rishi Sunak, have expressed similar support for "state aid" to left-behind regions.

Sanders, Warren, Brown, and other Democrats have embraced a new industrial policy on behalf of what Warren has called a new "economic patriotism." In Britain, Labour's Starmer will not go back to Tony Blair's acquiescence to Thatcher's big bang and privatization. Starmer has promised to build on the 2017 and 2019 manifestos. In the United States and Great Britain, the question is which version of "state aid" or "industrial policy" wins out. Will it be underlain by a renewed growth of the labor movement—which is particularly necessary in the United States, where labor represents only a tenth of the labor force? Will it entail a substantial redistribution of wealth and power?

As Erik Olin Wright argued in his last book, a socialist alternative does not for the time being have to be labeled "socialist." There are a host of politicians in the Democratic Party who are advocating democratic proposals that shift the balance of power in America toward working people and away from capital. There is very little support in the Democratic Party in the United States or the Labour Party of Great Britain for Clinton's or Blair's "third way." As the Business Roundtable's statement shows, business elites have lost their enthusiasm for market fundamentalism. Government will have to step in, and for those on the left, whether explicitly socialist or not, that will mean a chance to redress decades of rising inequality in wealth and power.

A successor to Sanders, who ran a viable presidential campaign as a democratic socialist, may not soon appear. But I think that for many of the young and soon-to-be middle-aged, and for a rising generation of politicians, support for "socialism"—in its post–Cold War iterations with the connotation of putting the interests of "society" above those of private enterprise—may eventually become how they describe the alternative to a failing free-market capitalism. The label "liberal" has become too closely identified with the extremes of social liberalism and identity politics. It has lost its mooring in New Deal economics. And "progressive" has always lacked content.

Of course, Americans could follow the lead of leftwing academics and decide to call their politics "social democratic," or they could devise an entirely new name. What matters is not the movement's name, but its collective aims. And these, the reclamation of public power over the direction of private enterprise and the rehabilitation of a decaying democracy, have become urgent in the wake of the pandemic and the economic depression.

Nicholas Lemann and Jimmy P. So did yeoman work as editors, helping me to explore a subject about which, in contrast to my other books, I knew too much and had too many unresolved complexes. I am looking forward again to working with Camille McDuffie and Miranda Sita on getting this book read, even in the midst of a pandemic. Rafe Sagalyn negotiated my contract. Sujay Kumar checked my facts.

I owe special thanks to my old friend Fred Block. Some of the ideas for this book germinated during breakfasts we had during semi-annual visits to Oakland. Fred also read and commented on an early draft, as did Ruy Teixeira, Dan Lewis, Bill Burr, Larry Lynn, and Michael Kazin. My friend in Madrid David Peck did an excellent job spotting errors in the final text.

I got advice on what to read and who to see and what to think from Richard Healey, Barbara Dudley, Barbara Epstein, Leo Casey, Sheri Berman, Albena Azmanova, David Duhalde, Bhaskar Sunkara, Nancy Fraser, James Cronin, Eric Foner, Thomas Edsall, Robin Blackburn, Miriam Bensman, Michael Lind, Jack Ross, Dustin Guastella, Harold Meyerson, Scott Horton, Robert Kuttner, Peggy Somers, Daniel Finn, Jonathan Haidt, Heather Gautney, Howard Gardner, Constance Flanagan, Stella Rouse, Jacob Swenson-Lengyel, and Max Blumenthal. Sean McElwee gave me access to very useful polling that YouGov had done for his organization, Data for Progress.

My family, Susan Pearson, Hilary Judis, and Eleanor Judis (who did some valuable research for me), kept me sane, no mean feat in these times, as did Max.

Many young people in the United States and Great Britain look favorably on socialism and even call themselves "socialists" without reading a word of Karl Marx's work. Ella Morton, the head of the Corvallis, Oregon, chapter of the Young Democratic Socialists of America, told an interviewer that she doesn't identify with the "economic part" of democratic socialism, but with the emphasis on "community bonds" and that she doesn't want to read Marx who, she fears, would "ruin democratic socialism" for her. But for someone trying to understand capitalism and socialism on a theoretical basis, Marx's and Engels's works are still the touchstone. The works I describe as "post-Marxist" arise out of an engagement with Marx's thought.

Marx's great work is *Capital*, Vol. I, which lays out his theory of capitalism and the transition from feudalism to capitalism. Marx describes the politics of the transition to socialism in *The Communist Manifesto* and *The Critique of the Gotha Program*. In "Socialism: Scientific and Utopian," Engels lays out his and Marx's differences with Robert Owen and the utopian socialists.

Two works that weaned me from Marx's precise stages of history were Karl Lowith's *Meaning in History* (Chicago, 1949) and Alec Nove's *The Economics of Feasible Socialism* (Taylor and Francis, 1983). I began to think about the possibility of socialism occurring within capitalism when I read the concluding essay of Martin J. Sklar's *The United States as a Developing Country* (Cambridge 1992). Sklar elaborates his theory in "Thoughts on Capitalism and Socialism: Realistic and Utopian," in *The Journal of the Gilded Age and Progressive Era*, October 2003.

Erik Olin Wright and G. A. Cohen were hard-core Marxists who in the last decades of their life broke with Marxist orthodoxy. In *Why Not Socialism?* (Princeton, 2009), Cohen makes a case for the moral basis of socialism. In *How to Be an Anti-Capitalist in the 21st Century* (Verso, 2019), Wright argues for creating socialist institutions within capitalism. Wright wrote a critical appreciation of Sklar's theory of the "mix" of capitalism and socialism in *Telos*, Spring 2019.

I first read Karl Polanyi's *The Great Transformation* (Beacon, 1980) sometime in the 1980s, and it had no impact on me. Under prodding from my friend Fred Block, I tried again about five years ago, and I was astonished at how relevant it is to understanding capitalism today. I highly recommend Block and Margaret Somers's book on Polanyi, *The Power of Market Fundamentalism* (Harvard, 2016). Robert Kuttner has a good summary of Polanyi's importance, "Karl Polanyi Explains It All," in the *American Prospect*, April 2014.

A good history of American socialism is Michael Kazin's *American Dreamers* (Random House, 2011). Jack Ross has written a comprehensive history, *The Socialist Party of America* (Potomac, 2015), which goes from Debs to DSA. Nick Salvatore's *Eugene Debs: Citizen and Socialist* (Illinois, 1982) is a superb biography. I first learned about Debs and the Socialist Party from James Weinstein, *The Decline of Socialism in America: 1912–1925,* (Monthly Review, 1967). For Christian socialism and its influence, I recommend Gary Dorrien's *The Soul in Society* (Fortress, 1995).

As readers will sense, my view of twentieth-century British history and of the Labour Party was heavily influenced by David Edgerton's *The Rise and Fall of the British Nation* (Penguin, 2018). I found Andrew Thorpe's *A History of the British Labour Party* (Red Globe, 2015) useful. Rosa Prince's *Comrade Corbyn* (Biteback, 2016) tells the story of the former Labour leader. David Kogan's *Protest and Power: The Battle for the Labour Party* (Bloomsbury, 2019) traces the conflict between Labour's factions from the 1970s to the present.

NOTES

INTRODUCTION

18 **In an October 2019 YouGov poll:** Fourth Annual Report on U.S. Attitudes Toward Socialism. Accessed at https://www.victimsofcommunism.org/2019-annual-poll.

21 **They included Philippe Buchez:** Gary Dorrien, *Soul in Society: The Making and Renewal of Social Christianity* (Fortress Press, 1995).

25 **Bernstein continued to embrace Marx's goal of socialism:** From Eduard Bernstein, *Evolutionary Socialism* (1899).

27 **Martin J. Sklar contended that the competitive capitalism of Marx's days:** Martin J. Sklar, *The United States as a Developing Country* (Cambridge, 1992), p. 214.

27 **the first steps of progress along the long and difficult path:** Axel Honneth, *The Idea of Socialism: Towards a Renewal* (Polity, 2017).

28 **Alternative, noncapitalist economic activities:** Erik Olin Wright, *How to Be an Anti-Capitalist in the 21st Century* (Verso, 2019).

28 **"there is no single moment of transition from a profit-oriented economy to a socialist economy":** Fred Block,

"Financial Democratization and the Transition to Socialism," prepared for workshop on "Democratizing Finance" at the University of Wisconsin, May–June 2018.

29 **"The moment anyone started to talk to Marx about morality, he would roar with laughter":** Quoted in Steven Lukes, *Marxism and Morality* (Clarendon, 1985), p. 27.

29 **"It is commonly true on camping trips":** G.A. Cohen, *Why Not Socialism* (Princeton, 2009).

33 **What is now in crisis is a whole conception of socialism:** Ernesto Laclau and Chantal Mouffe *Hegemony and Socialist Strategy* (1985).

34 **appealed to socialist values as the means to unite a majority:** G. A. Cohen, "Back to Socialist Basics," *New Left Review*, September–October, 1994.

CHAPTER ONE

42 **"out of darkness into light":** Many of Debs's speeches are collected in an internet archive: https://www.marxists.org/archive/debs/index.htm.

42 **"They took their socialism like a new religion":** Cited in Michael Kazin, *American Dreamers: How the Left Changed a Nation* (Vintage, 2012).

134 45 "Socialism is an eschatological movement": See Daniel Bell, "The Problem of Ideological Rigidity," *The End of Ideology: On the Exhaustion of Political Ideas in the Fifties* (1960).

50 in 1970 that there were 35,800 hippies in Vermont: Cited in Harry Jaffe, *Why Bernie Sanders Matters* (Regan Arts, 2015).

50 The Revolution is coming, and it is a very beautiful revolution: *Freeman*, November 1969.

51 Sanders campaigned as a socialist: *Seven Days*, December 12, 1972.

51 "that idea suddenly becomes acceptable reality": *Seven Days*, 1976.

51 "No one gives a damn about your ideology": Tim Murphy, "How Bernie Sanders Learned to Be a Real Politician," *Mother Jones*, May 26, 2015.

52 "make it into a modern corporation": Quoted in Jaffe, *Why Bernie Sanders Matters*.

52 a "Eugene V. Debs type of socialist": *Atlantic*, October 5, 2015 (publication of unpublished profile from 1985).

52 "If you ask me if the banks should be nationalized, I would say yes": *Baltimore Sun*, November 23, 1981.

52–53 "I'm not afraid of government control in economics": *Rutland Herald,* April 28, 1988

53 "the guts to raise the issues that all of us know to be true": Speech reprinted in *Monthly Review*, November 1989.

53 "as it exists in countries such as Sweden": *Burlington Free Press*, October 16, 1990.

53 Asked to define his kind of socialism: *Rutland Daily Herald,* November 3, 1990.

54 "socialism doesn't mean state ownership of everything": Associated Press, November 7, 1990.

54 "democracy and socialism can exist in a compatible way": *Rutland Daily Herald,* June 8, 1988.

54 socialism as a command economy of nationalized firms was dashed: *Washington Post*, May 2, 2019.

57 "give workers an ownership stake in the companies they work for": "Corporate Accountability and Democracy," Bernie Sanders homepage. Accessed at https://berniesanders.com/issues/corporate-accountability-and-democracy/.

57 "it's too late to do anything inside the Beltway": Andrew Prokop, "Bernie Sanders's Political Revolution, Explained," Vox,

January 28, 2016. Accessed at
https://www.vox.com/2016/1
/28/10853502/bernie-sanders
-political-revolution.

57   **historian Eric Foner penned
an open letter to Sanders:** Eric
Foner, *Nation*, October 21, 2015.

58   **the need to rein in the
excesses of capitalism:** See the
campaign memoir of Sanders
aide Heather Gautney, *Crashing
the Party: From the Bernie Sanders
Campaign to a Progressive Movement*
(Verso, 2018).

61   **"we're talking about
countries and systems that
already exist":** Nisha Stickles
and Barbara Corbellini Duarte,
"Exclusive: Alexandria Ocasio-
Cortez explains what democratic
socialism means to her," *Business
Insider*, March 4, 2019. Accessed
at https://www.businessinsider
.com/alexandria-ocasio-cortez
-explains-what-democratic
-socialism-means-2019
-3?utm_source=markets&utm
_medium=ingest.

CHAPTER TWO

65   **43 percent of Democrats had
a favorable view of socialism:**
Peter Moore, "One Third of
Millennials View Socialism
Favorably," YouGov, May 11, 2015.
Accessed at https://today.yougov
.com/topics/politics/articles
-reports/2015/05/11/one-third
-millennials-like-socialism.

67   **47 percent preferred
socialism:** Data for Progress,
Progressive Future of the Party.

68   **those who thought of
themselves as socialists were very
likely to live in a city or suburb:**
Compiled by author from data sets
provided by YouGov and Data for
Progress.

68   **voted for Democrats in
roughly the same proportion:**
John B. Judis and Ruy Teixeira,
The Emerging Democratic Majority
(Scribner, 2002).

69   **The rest of the alternatives
were a grab bag:** Frank Newport,
"The Meaning of 'Socialism' to
Americans Today," Polling
Matters (Gallup), October 4, 2018.
Accessed at https://news.gallup.com
/opinion/polling-matters/243362
/meaning-socialism-americans
-today.aspx.

70   **Over half think it will pose a
"serious threat" in their lifetimes:**
RJ Reinhart, "Global Warming Age
Gap: Younger Americans Most
Worried," Gallup, May 11, 2018.
Accessed at https://news.gallup
.com/poll/234314/global-warming
-age-gap-younger-americans
-worried.aspx.

71   **gap in income between a male
high school graduate:** Kevin Drum,
"Chart of the Day: The College
Wage Premium over Time," *Mother
Jones*, August 9, 2019. Accessed at
https://www.motherjones.com

136 /kevin-drum/2019/08/chart-of
-the-day-the-college-wage
-premium-over-time/.

71 **Average student debt for the young rose:** Kevin Drum, "Chart of the Day: The College Wage Premium over Time."

72 **One survey of 40 Uber drivers:** Katie Wells, Kafui Attoh, and Declan Cullen, "The Uber Workplace in D.C.: Georgetown University," Kalmanovitz Initiative for Labor and the Working Poor, 2019.

72 **before they could afford to buy a house:** Alexis Madrigal, "Why Housing Policy Feels Like Generational Warfare," *Atlantic*. June 13, 2019.

72 **According to a McKinsey Study in 2013:** Accessed at https:// www.mckinsey.com/~/media /mckinsey/industries/social%20 sector/our%20insights/voice%20 of%20the%20graduate/voice_of _the_graduate.ashx.

75 **When Bhaskar Sunkara went to his first DSA meeting in 2007:** "The ABCs of Jacobin," *Columbia Journalism Review*, January 2, 2019.

77 **DSA's membership of approximately 70,000:** These estimates are based on conversations with David Duhalde, who was deputy director of the organization, and had access to the survey numbers, which he quoted to me.

81 **"DSA should make it clear that we will not endorse corporate politicians":** Andrew Sernatinger, "If Sanders Should Lose," *Medium*, July 19, 2019. Accessed at https://medium .com/@andrew.sernatinger/if -sanders-should-lose-e1559c7 b2fd3.

81 **'What did you do in the war against the neofascist Donald Trump?':** Harold Meyerson, "What the Socialists Just Did— and Why," *American Prospect*, August 9, 2019. Accessed at https://prospect.org/power /socialists-just-did-and/.

82 **"We believe Biden's anti- Chinese xenophobic messaging & the allegations of sexual assault":** https://twitter.com/DemSocialists /status/1260244691888504834 ?s=20.

84 **political scientist Lee Drutman found in his survey of the 2016 election:** Lee Drutman, "Political Divisions in 2016 and Beyond," Voter Study Group, June 2017.

86 **"new breed of American democratic socialists is simply advocating a model that embraces government's important role":** Joseph Stiglitz, "A 'democratic socialist' agenda is appealing. No wonder Trump attacks it," *Washington Post*, May 18, 2019.

87 rethink the markets-first approach in favor of a pragmatic assessment: "New Rules for the Twenty-First Century: Corporate Power, Public Power, and the Future of the American Economy," The Roosevelt Institute. Accessed at https://www.new-rules-for-the-21st-century.com/.

89 She's really a democratic socialist in some ways: Steven Rattner, "The Warren Way Is the Wrong Way," *New York Times*, November 4, 2019. Accessed at https://www.nytimes.com/2019/11/04/opinion/medicare-warren-plan.html.

89 When one writer suggested that he sounded like Debs: George Packer, "The Throwback Democrat," *Atlantic*, February 7, 2019. Accessed at https://www.theatlantic.com/ideas/archive/2019/02/sherrod-brown-just-what-democrats-need-2020/582208/.

CHAPTER THREE

93 they were not enamored of actual working-class ownership and control: "Socialism: the Fabian Essays," Boston, 1894.

93 "the pessimism of the revolutionaries": John Maynard Keynes, "Economic Possibilities for our Grandchildren," 1930.

94 A mixed economy is what most people of the West would prefer: Quoted in David Marquand,

Britain Since 1918: The Strange Career of British Democracy (Orion, 2009).

96 "owes much more to the teachings of Jesus": Tony Benn, "Revolutionary Christianity," *Marxism Today,* January, 1980.

96 Benn outlined a plan for "industrial democracy": Reprinted in *The Best of Benn: Speeches, Diaries, Letters, and Other Writings* (Hutchinson, 2014).

98 "brokers, jobbers, and the City's traditional merchant banks merged": BBC News, October 27, 2016.

100 "brought a deterioration in public-sector service standards and democratic accountability": Robin Blackburn, "The Corbyn Project," *New Left Review*, May–June 2018.

102 "I think it's called socialism": Quote from Richard Seymour, *Corbyn: The Strange Rebirth of Radical Politics* (Verso, 2016).

102 hoping to "break the grip of the Blairites": Quote from Richard Seymour: *Corbyn: The Strange Rebirth of Radical Politics.*

103 as "a coalition of idealistic youngsters": *Conversation,* September 12, 2015.

103 "moral sense of purpose rooted in Methodism": Rosa Prince, *Comrade Corbyn* (Biteback, 2016).

138

105   his positions were more in line with Benn's socialism: Quote from "John McDonnell: The Self-Made Socialist," *Prospect*, September 18, 2018.

108   being a teenager in late capitalist Britain is now: Mark Fisher, *Capitalist Realism: Is There No Alternative?* (Zero Books, 2009).

110   Most scientists would regard 2030 as a radical and probably unattainable target: On the more standard view by social scientists and scientists, see https://www.foreignaffairs.com/articles/2020-04-13/paths-net-zero and https://prospect.org/greennewdeal/getting-to-a-carbon-free-economy/.

113   When I knocked on your doors in 2017: Laura Pidcock, "Letter to the People I Represented," *Medium*, December 18, 2019. Accessed at https://medium.com/@laura.pidcock.mp/letter-to-the-people-i-represented-406aea893243.

113   Convincing an electoral majority in the grip of post-crash austerity: Steve Hall and Simon Winlow, "Back to the Future: On the British Liberal Left's Return to Origins" (draft).

115   "The democratic nation and its rule of law is the best means of safeguarding our rights and freedoms": Jonathan Rutherford, "Blue Labour has been tragically vindicated," *Medium*, December 14, 2019. Accessed at https://medium.com/@blue_labour/blue-labour-has-been-tragically-vindicated-38022a970f9a.

116   "is that we are all Keynesians now": "The Guardian View on Boris Johnson's Budget: We Are All Keynesians Now," *Guardian*, March 11, 2020. Accessed at https://www.theguardian.com/commentisfree/2020/mar/11/the-guardian-view-on-boris-johnsons-budget-we-are-all-keynesians-now.

116   "a rational choice for the wrong reasons": Yanis Varoufakis, "Yanis Varoufak Is on Brexit: A Rational Choice for the Wrong Reasons," *Financial News of London*, February 25, 2020. Accessed at https://www.fnlondon.com/articles/yanis-varoufakis-on-brexit-a-rational-choice-for-the-wrong-reasons-20200225.

CONCLUSION

119   It obscures the leading role of nurses and schoolteachers: Meagan Day, "Bernie Sanders and Elizabeth Warren Aren't Playing the Same Game," *Jacobin*, August 2019. Accessed at https://www.jacobinmag.com/2019/08/bernie-sanders-elizabeth-warren-democratic-party-elite-2020-presidential-race.

120   Sunkara quotes Luxemburg: Bhaskar Sunkara, *The Socialist*

Manifesto: The Case for Radical Politics in an Era of Extreme Inequality (Verso, 2019).

120 **"There Is No Left Case for Nationalism":** Atossa Araxia Abrahamian, "There Is No Left Case for Nationalism," *Nation*, November 28, 2018.

120 **Blue Labour's support for national identity has been branded "bigoted":** Chloe Chaplain, "What is Blue Labour, the controversial 'culturally conservative' group calling for support to shape the future of the party?" *i*, December 16, 2019.

120 **"There is a simple reason why pandering to nationalism will, in the end, always benefit the right":** Sabrina Huck, "Labour must reject nationalism for an inclusive definition of community," LabourList, March 3, 2020.

120 **only 12.3 percent of the respondents described themselves as "patriotic":** https://twitter.com/DavidKlion/status/1258026745128722432?s=20.

123 **"should be conceivable within the lifespan of one generation":** Alec Nove, *The Economics of Feasible Socialism* (Allen & Unwin, 1983).

126 **began a series of articles calling for a "reset of capitalism":** "Financial Times Launches First Campaign Since Global Financial Crisis," B2B marketing, September 24, 2019. Accessed at https://www.b2bmarketing.net/en/resources/news/financial-times-launches-first-campaign-global-financial-crisis.